ADOBE PHOTOSHOP 2024 USER'S GUIDE FOR ALL USERS

A COMPLETE STEP-BY-STEP ILLUSTRATED GUIDE TO MASTERING ADOBE PHOTOSHOP ELEMENT 2024 WITH UPDATED TIPS, TRICKS AND SHORTCUTS.

PETER JOHN

LEGAL NOTICE

TABLE OF CONTENT

vi

INTRODUCTION

The Adobe Photoshop Element is aimed at a wide range of users, including amateur photographers, professional designers, and graphics artists, who want to get their hands on high-quality tools for editing, generating graphics, and cataloging.

The truth is that finding the program that best meets your needs is not as stressful as you think. You've discovered what you're searching for with Adobe Photoshop Element.

Although advanced and intricate, Adobe Photoshop Element 2024's capabilities are easy to learn. Additionally, no prior technical knowledge is required to install Photoshop Element on your PC.

But let's start at the beginning of this user manual and go over how to use all of Photoshop Elements' amazing features.

Make sure your computer is running as efficiently as possible and that your internet connection is stable to get the most out of this user manual.

I hope you have luck as you go through this user handbook.

I'll see you in the following segment.

CHAPTER ONE

GETTING ACQUAINTED WITH ADOBE PHOTOSHOP ELEMENT 2024

Adobe Photoshop Element is a graphic editing software designed by the Adobe computer software community and used by photographers, videographers, image editors, graphic designers, and anyone who desires to edit and create their photos or videos. The Adobe Photoshop Element allows its users to create, organize, make changes to images, and share them with other platforms like **Email, Flickr, Twitter, Vimeo, and YouTube.**

The first version of Adobe Photoshop Elements was released in April 2001 and initially targeted at casual photographers. It was later developed and upgraded to carry out a wider scope of digital functions for its users.

Adobe Photoshop Element is a one-time purchase that does not require a periodic subscription to keep the software running. AI-powered one-click subject selection, content-aware crop, automatic image colorization, and skin smoothness are some of the many tools available in the Adobe Photoshop Element. It is available for use on both Mac and Windows.

Adobe Photoshop Element 2024

The Adobe Photoshop Element 2024, like its previous and earlier versions, is a graphic editing software, designed to create and edit digital files like photos, images, and videos

1

but better enhanced with new features for an effective user experience. It provides an easy way to get started, with guidelines on how to effortlessly create stunning image creations, effects, designs, prints, etc. This version is the latest version of Adobe Photoshop Elements and it was launched on the 19th of October, 2023.

Exploring The New Features in Adobe Photoshop Elements 2024.

New astounding features for better performance than the earlier versions of Photoshop Element have been added to the 2024 version of Adobe Photoshop Elements., Now let`s explore the new features powered by Adobe Sensei like the earlier versions of Photoshop Elements.

- **Match Color and Tone**: One of the new features introduced by Adobe Photoshop Element is the Match Color and Tone feature. With this feature, you can select colors and tones from built-in presets or your own images of photos.

- **Create Stylized Text:** With the Add Text Guided Edit, your text can be aligned horizontally, vertically or on a path, selection or a shape. You can use the gradient, textures, and patterns to wrap or style your text. To access this feature, open your photos, go to **Basic**, click **Guided Mode** and then click on **Add Text**. Here you can follow the steps to select from the options made available.

- **Free Access of Adobe Stock:** With this feature, you can easily gain access to thousands of free Adobe Stock photos. You can use the free Adobe Stock photo to replace your background image. The Adobe Stock can also be accessed from the Quote Graphics. Go to the **File** menu, click on the **Search on Adobe Stock,** and search for the desired image in the library

- **Quick Actions:** This feature allows you to make one-click edits to your images. With this feature, you make selections on your background for simple modifications, remove JPEG fragments to make photos sharper, and instantly add color to old photos. To access this feature, open any of your photos and click on the **Quick Action** panel in the **Quick Mode**

- **Photo Reels: This is another powerful feature that comes with Element 2024.** This feature allows you to display your best photos exceptionally. To access this feature, open your images, click Create, and select **Photo Reel.** Finally, you can select a layout from the sizes options available**.**

- **Web and Mobile Companion Apps:** Photoshop Element 2024 comes with a web and mobile app. This feature allows you to make quick edits and adjustments from your devices which can be uploaded easily to the Cloud. The web app allows you to create a slide show, modern collages, creative patterns for texts, etc.

2

The Adobe Photoshop Element 2024 System Requirement On Windows And Mac.

Putting the horse before the cart, the first thing to determine is whether your Windows or Mac system has what it takes to operate Adobe Photoshop Element 2023 before downloading and installing it on your computer. This goes without saying that this software now has a few new and sophisticated functions, which is another reason you should know in advance if your Windows and Mac are capable of running it. It is also important to know that The Adobe Photoshop Element Software application is not supported on Windows 8

The minimal system requirements for Photoshop 2021 on Windows and Mac are shown below.

Windows

Minimum Requirement

- Intel 6th Generation or newer processor or AMD equivalent with SSE4.1 support
- Microsoft Windows 10 (version 22H2) or Windows 11 (version 22H2), 64-bit versions only; Windows 7, Windows 8.1 not supported
- 8 GB of RAM
- 8 GB of available hard disk space to install the application; additional space required for downloading online content and for temporary files during product installation and usage (cannot install on a volume that uses a case-sensitive file system or on removable flash storage devices)
- 1280 x 800 display resolution (at 100% scale factor)
- Microsoft DirectX 12 compatible display driver
- Internet connection required for product activation and download of features and online content

macOS

Minimum Requirement

- Intel 6th Generation or newer processor; Apple silicon M1 or newer processor
- macOS 12, macOS 13 (13.4 or later)
- 8 GB of RAM
- 6 GB of available hard disk space to install the application; additional space required for downloading online content and for temporary files during product

installation and usage (cannot install on a volume that uses a case-sensitive file system or on removable flash storage devices)

- 1280 x 800 display resolution (at 100% scale factor)
- Internet connection required for product activation and download of features and online content

Downloading and installing The Adobe Photoshop Element 2024

After learning the minimal and recommended system requirements for downloading and installing Adobe Photoshop Elements, you can start the download. However, before you do, consider the below, be sure;

- You have the most recent version of Internet Explorer, Firefox, Chrome, or Safari and administrative rights for your account.
- You've removed pop-up blockers in your web browser and temporarily turned off firewalls, antivirus programs, and third-party security software. By doing this, You may speed up the installation process
- You have an administrative privilege for the account you are using.
- You also have a valid Adobe ID.
- You have a valid serial number for Photoshop Elements.
- You are connected to the internet to finalize the installation.

Downloading The Adobe Photoshop Elements 2023

Follow the procedures below to download the Adobe Photoshop Elements

- On your web browser page, enter the URL link to download the Adobe Photoshop Elements *https://helpx.adobe.com/download-install/kb/photoshop-elements-downloads.html*
- Then click on **Download** for either **Windows** or **Mac**

For Windows	For macOS
Download 64-bit	Download
Languages: Czech, Dutch, English, French, German, Italian, Japanese, Polish, Spanish, and Swedish	**Languages:** English, French, German, and Japanese

Installing The Adobe Photoshop Element 2024

After successfully downloading the Photoshop Element on your PC, the next step is to install it.

- ◆ Launch Adobe Photoshop Element installer on your computer.
- ◆ Sign in using your Adobe ID.
- ◆ Click Continue on the following screen that pops up.
- ◆ On **the Installation Options** screen, click on **Select language** and **Specify installation location,** and select **Continue**

In the next screen that appears, select your previous version of Photoshop Element and then click on **Confirm**

✦ In the next screen that pops up, **Launch The Photo Editor** to load the Adobe Photoshop Editor Workspace.

✦ Then sign in again using your **Adobe ID** and **password**

7

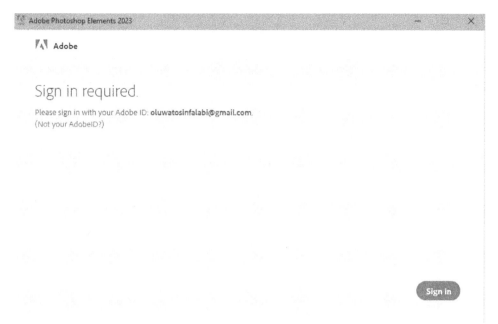

- On the next page, click on **Activate Now** on the **Welcome screen**

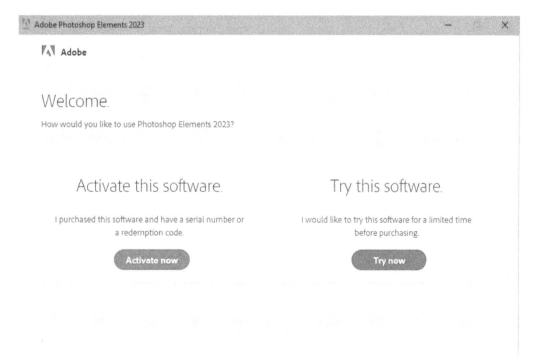

- In the next screen, enter the serial number and click on **Next.**

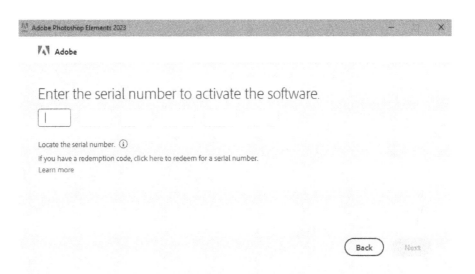

Here the Photo Editor is launched successfully.

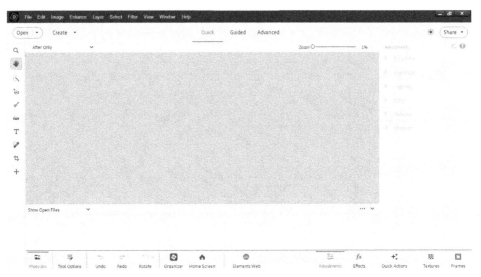

CHAPTER TWO

LEARNING THE BASICS OF IMAGE EDITING

Getting Acquainted with The Home Screen

The first thing that comes into view after downloading and installing Photoshop Element 2024 on your PC

Home Screen.

The Home Screen contains auto-generated photos, videos, and slide shows customized by the software for its users making do with the imported media.

You can find entertaining editing projects, gather creative inspiration, switch workspaces, access recently opened files, and ask the Adobe community for assistance from the home screen.

Let's quickly go through the major icons on the Home Screen.

- ⬧ **The Search Bar**: This can be used to rapidly search for Help documents and tutorials for various features; it is positioned at the top of the Home Screen. Enter the keyword you're looking for in the search bar, then hit Enter on your keyboard.

The relevant results will be shown in this location on the Home Screen as thumbnails and hyperlinks.

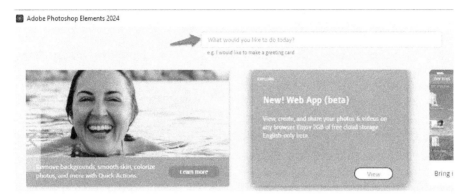

✦ **The Carousel of Cards:** The Home Screen's upper portion contains a carousel of cards that provide access to details about new features, tasks to do, and inspirational ideas. By clicking the arrows that appear on the carousel's right and left sides, you can go through it.

Some of the elements frequently found in the carousel are listed below:

☐ **Explore**: This tag allows you to tour around certain features in the Photoshop Element application. To access this feature, click on the **View** button.

☐
☐
☐ **What`s New:** Information on new features in the Photoshop Element application is provided by this blue tag. Click the **Open Link** button to access these resources.

☐ **Try This:** This tag is green and gives you access to a variety of intriguing features. Based on the actions you do and the features you use in Photoshop Elements, these features are shown and periodically updated. Click the **Try** button to try any of these features.

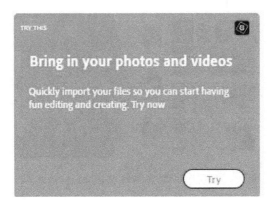

- **Auto Creations:** These can be found at the bottom of the Home Screen and are generated regularly by the software using the media that has been imported into the Elements. By selecting **Add media** from the Auto Creation menu, you can add media to **Auto Creations**. By selecting **View all** or the number icon beneath the Auto Creations thumbnail, you may view all the auto-created projects, including picture collages, slideshows, and video collages.

- **The Organizer:** The Organizer is located on the right-hand side of the Home Screen. This is where you import, browse, and arrange photographs to maintain the effectiveness and organization of your image collection. Tools for tagging, rating, sorting, and finding your photographs are available in the Organizer.

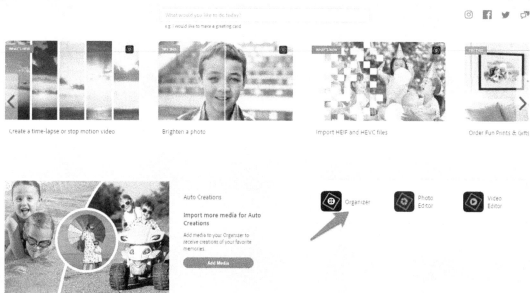

* **The Photo Editor:** The tools for making and altering photographs are included here. These include tools for brightness, color, adding effects, fixing images, etc.

* **The Video Editor:** This gives you access to Photoshop Element's videos and editing tools.

* **Recent Files:** On the Home Screen, you can access the project files that have recently been worked on here. You can immediately continue working on the

14

project from where you left it by using this symbol. Any open image in this window is seen in the Photo Editor.

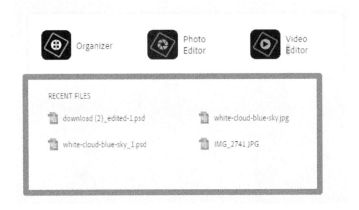

Launching The Photo Editor

The Photo Editor is one of the most crucial tools in the Photoshop Element. As was already mentioned, the Photo Editor has options for applying effects, adjusting brightness and color, fixing photographs, and more.

To open the Photo Editor in the Photoshop Element.

- ⬦ From the **Home Screen Interface**, click on **Photo Editor** from the right-hand side of the screen.

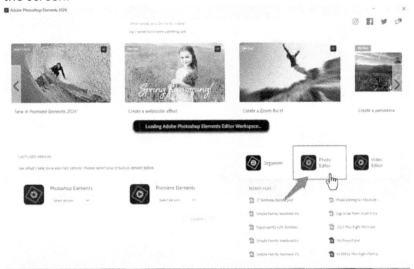

- ⬦ The main interface for the Photo Editor, which has a variety of tools for producing and modifying photographs, is depicted on the following page.

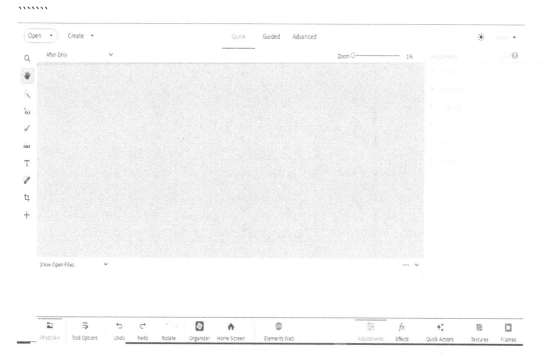

The Photo Editor is in Quick mode if the Quick tab is selected by default at the top of the workspace along with the other modes (**Guided and Advanced formerly known as Expert**). However, there aren't many controls available in Quick mode to change the brightness, color, contrast, and sharpness.

The workspace is divided into three editing modes: Quick, Guided, and Advanced. The Adjustments panel is docked in the area referred to as the panel Bin on the workspace's right side. The Tools panel is located on the left side of the workspace. When paired with objects in the Panel Bin and the tools within, the Tools panel offers an extensive array of options for editing, improving, and stylizing photos. Later in this book, the overview of the workspace will be addressed in detail.

Making Basic Edits In Elements` Quick Mode

Quick Edit is one of the Photo Editor's editing modes; it offers fewer possibilities than Expert Edit. The only tools accessible in the Toolbox's Quick Edit mode are the **Zoom Tool**, the **Hand Tool**, the **Selection Tools**, the **Healing Brush Tools**, the **Red Eye Removal Tool**, the **Whiten Teeth**, the **Straighten Tool**, the **Text Tools**, the **Healing Brush Tools**, the **Crop Tool**, and the **Move Tool**. All of these tools function in the same way in the Edit modes (whether in Quick or Advanced mode).

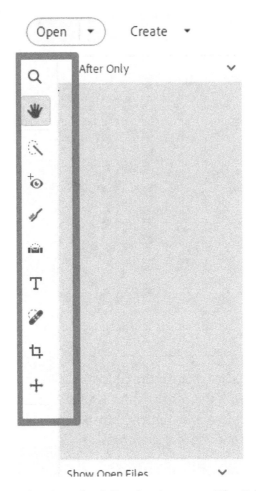

The Quick Edit mode Menu bar has the following buttons: File, Edit, Enhance, layer, filter, View Windows, and Help. Certain functions are marked as unavailable in the Menu bar and cannot be selected or accessed; this is shown by their gray display. Included in this is the Layer Menu

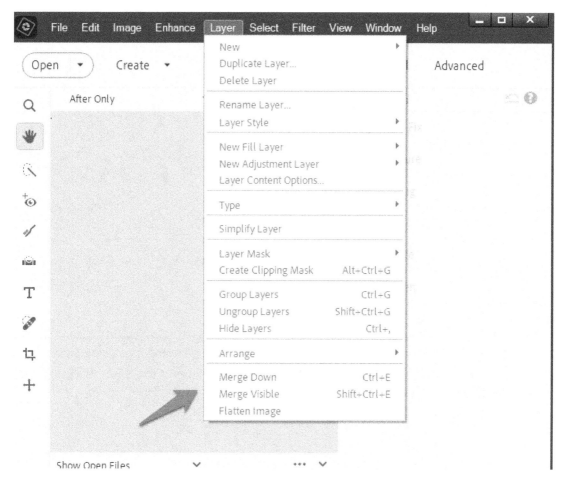

The **Panel Bin** is another feature in the Quick Edit mode. This feature contains tools such as **Photo Bin**, **Tool Options**, **Undo**, **Redo**, **Rotate**, **Organizer**, **Element Web**, **Adjustment**, **Effects**, **Quick Action**s, **Textures**, and **Frames**

To make edits and changes in Quick Edit Mode

- ❖ Launch the **Photo Editor** and be sure that the **Quick** tab is selected at the top of the screen.
- ❖ Click on a file from **Windows Explorer** or the **Mac Finder** to open it in Elements.
- ❖ Navigate to the desired file on your hard drive, pick it, then click **Open** in the resulting **Open dialog** box.

✦ Then, select Before & After-Horizontal from the View drop-down list.

✦ Make the necessary adjustments to your photo by cropping it or using Smart Fix.
✦ then select **File**, **Save As**, give the picture a new name in the **Save As** dialog box, and finally click **Save**.

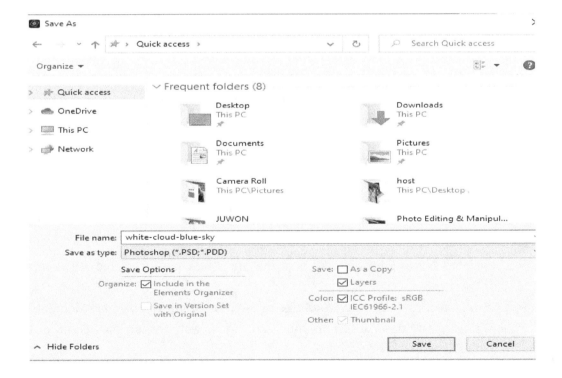

Sharing A Photo

The Adobe Photoshop Element 2024 is an amazing packaging tool that allows you to share media files (photos, videos, and projects) online using diverse platforms like Flickr, Facebook, Twitter, etc. Aside from being able to share single photo files online, you can also share the below.

- **Albums**: You can make an album with multiple images in it to share or upload on other websites.
- **Slideshow**: You also have the option to construct a slideshow and export it as a movie file (.wmv) or a PDF. Before uploading or sharing slideshows online, you can also include audio files.
- **Video files**: Adobe Element also allows you to upload videos for online viewing on many websites.

Photo Sharing Providers On Photoshop Element

You can post or share your images on a huge number of photo-sharing websites. However, Photoshop Element is connected to a few specific photo-sharing websites. The web pages on Photoshop Element are listed below.

- **Behance**: This is a site where you can showcase your artistic endeavors and view lovely designs and photography created by others.
- **DotPhoto**: This is an additional website where users may share images, however using it costs money for a club membership.
- **Facebook**: This is a social media platform for sharing unlimited photos and videos. Here on this platform, you sign up for an account.
- **Flickr**: This is a photo-sharing platform and social network where users upload photos for others to see. This is certainly one of the best online photo management and sharing applications in the world, and it allows 1TB of photo upload without limits.
- **Google +**: This is also an online platform where you can share photos with unlimited storage. Not only that, but you can also search for images uploaded by other users
- **Photobucket**: This is an easy-to-use and powerful platform where you share, host, and share images. You can share up to 2GB of photos and videos per month
- **Shutterfly**: This platform is concerned with creating photo books, wall art, photo cards, invitations, personalized gifts, calendars, etc.

- **SlicPic**: This is a platform for users to create beautiful, professional portfolio websites and galleries without coding. This platform makes it easy to display, share and grow your images online. You can store 200 size-limited images for the free account but for the paid account, you can get 50 GB of space and up with no limit size limits.
- **SmugMug**: This is a photo-sharing website that permits its users to store, share and sell their photos online. The amount to be paid for an account on this platform is a minimum of $3.84 per month.
- **Twitter**: This is also another platform for photo-sharing up to 100 images, with a max of 3MB each. Here on this website, recently uploaded pictures are displayed for all to see
- **Vimeo**: This a video-sharing platform that allows users to create high-quality videos to share with their audience with ease.
- **YouTube**: This is a free video-sharing website where you get to watch online videos, create yours, and even upload them online to share.

Sharing Photos On Element

Organizer and the **Photo Editor** are the two applications on the Home Screen to share photos.

Sharing Photo files with The Organizer

Follow the step-by-step guide below to learn how to share photos using the Organizer.

- Launch the **Organizer** from the **Home Screen**

- Click on **Media** and select the picture you desire to share when the **Organizer** opens.

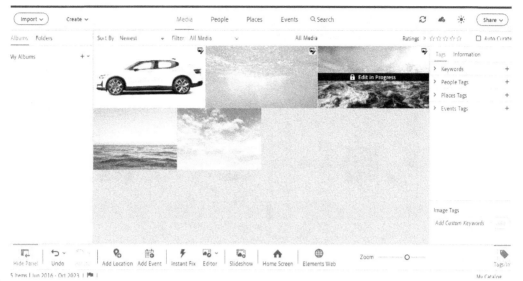

✦ Click on **Share** and select an option from the **Share** drop-down menu.

22

Sharing Photos with The Photo Editor

Follow the step-by-step guide below to learn how to share photos using the Photo Editor

- ◆ **Open** the **Photo Editor** from the **Home Screen**

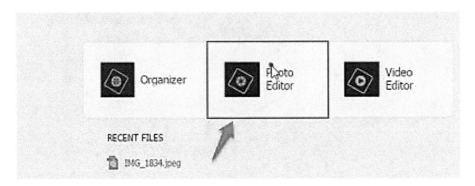

- ◆ When the **Photo Editor** opens, select the picture you wish to share
- ◆ Click on **Share** and select an option from the **Share** drop-down menus

Retracing Your Steps

There will be moments when you will make a mistake while you are altering your photographs or you will just not like the modification you have made. You may easily retrace your steps by using the Undo and Redo commands.

- ◆ Go to **Edit** in the **Menu bar** and select **Undo (Ctrl + Z)** or **Redo (Ctrl + Y)** to utilize the command.

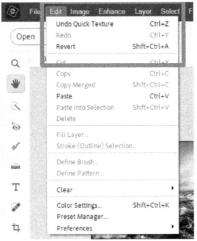

The History panel

Visualizing the editing history of an image or project is made easier with the help of the History panel. You can navigate around the History panel to make changes during the current work session, and it provides a comprehensive list of all the modifications that have been made to the picture or photo.

The History panel can be opened following the steps below:

- ✦ Go to **Windows** and select **History** to launch the **History** panel. Then you see the list of editings that have been made.

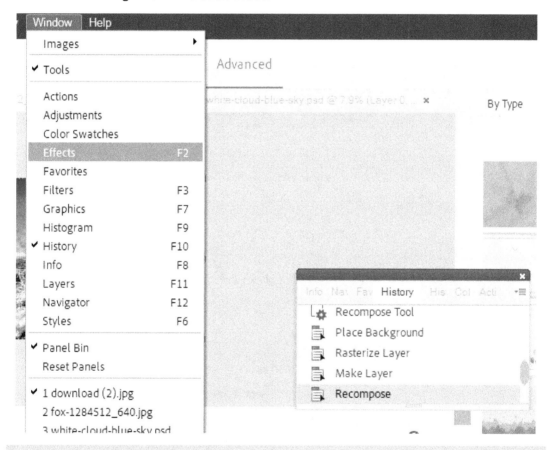

Reverting To A Previous State Of An Image.

To return to the previous state of an image, in both the Quick and Expert modes, three simple ways can be used, and they are stated below.

- ✦ **Method A:** Click on the state in the History Panel

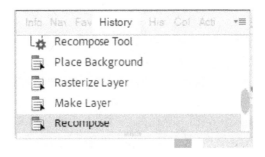

♦ **Method B:** Use the **Undo** or **Redo** button in the **Taskbar**

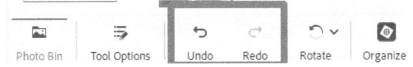

♦ **Method C:** Using the **Undo** and **Redo** in the **Edit Menu**

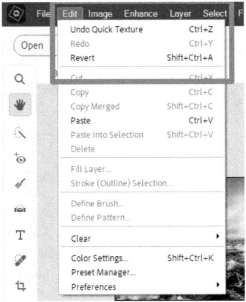

Reverting to The Last Save

When you use the Revert command, all edits and modifications are undone and the image is restored to its previous state. To undo any

♦ Go to the **Edit Menu** and select **Revert**

Erasing And Deleting States From The History panel

To remove any modification in the list you no longer want in your image, do the following

- ✦ Right-click on the action and select **Delete**
- ✦ Then select **Yes** from the menu bar that pops up to approve the deletion.

The procedures below can be used to remove the list of states from the History panel without altering the visual.

- ✦ Right-click on the action and select **Clear History**
- ✦ Then click **Ok to confirm the deletion**

Pay attention to the guidelines below while using the History panel:

- ✦ The History panel only shows the last 50 states by default; any additional states that surpass 50 are automatically erased to make room for Photoshop Element. The maximum number of states is 1000, however, you can customize the number to anything you choose. Follow these steps to accomplish this:

- Select **Preference** from the **Edit** menu, then click **Performance**.

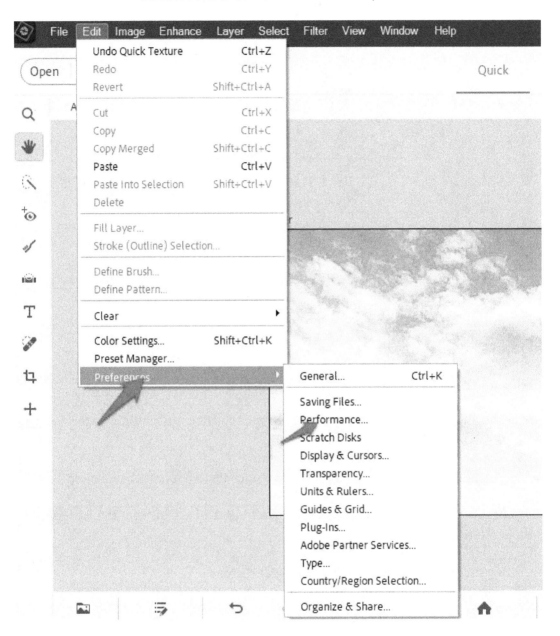

- Change the stats number to what you want in the **Performance** tab's **History** & **Cache** section, and then click "Ok."

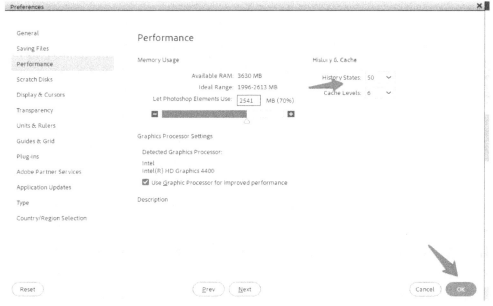

- The element uses more memory the more states you keep in your History panel.
- The original condition of the photo is always shown at the very top of the History panel. Simply clicking on the top state will restore the image to its original form.
- The name of the tool or command used to change the image is listed next to each state in the History panel.
- The oldest state is at the top of the History panel list, while the most recent state is at the bottom.
- The states in the History panel are all removed after you close a document.
- All the states that follow the state you choose when you alter the image. Additionally, when a state is deleted, all the states that follow it are also deleted.
- The previous states are dimmed when you choose one, so you can choose the state that will be ignored while working with the chosen state.

Getting A Helping Hand

When utilizing your Photoshop Element, you may encounter problems and need help. Here are other tools that Adobe has made available for use in similar situations.

The Help Menu

The Help menu, which aids in accessing the Photoshop Help menu, is the first place to look.

At the top of the Photo Editor or Organizer interface, next to the other menus, is where you'll find the **Help** menu.

When you select the **Help** menu, the commands are presented, and from them, you can get the information you need.

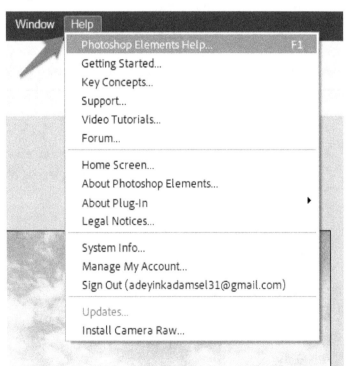

Now let's check out some of the commands in the Help menu

- ✦ **Photoshop Element Help:** Here's a search box where you can type in a topic to get a list of search results. You can press the shortcut key F1 to access the Element Help file.
- ✦ **Getting Started:** When you want advice and information on how to get started in Elements, this command is useful.
- ✦ **Key Concepts:** When you see a phrase or word that you don't understand, this command can be helpful. When you choose this option, a web page opens and your default web browser is instantly launched, bringing up numerous web pages that define the important ideas.
- ✦ **Support:** You can access the Adobe website by using this command to launch your web browser. You may find up-to-date details regarding Elements, user-reported issues, and some helpful advice for using the Adobe Element on the Adobe website. Numerous resources on the Adobe website will facilitate and improve the use of Adobe Elements and offer numerous fixes for any issues that may arise.
- ✦ **Video Tutorial:** You can use this command to open a web page on Adobe's website that has videos to assist you in utilizing the Adobe Element.
- ✦ **Forum:** This command takes you to a page where you may view user comments and queries with solutions to typical issues that arise when using the Element.

The Tooltips

When you hover your mouse over any object in the Photoshop Element, more help resources will appear as text below your cursor. The texts that appear provide descriptions of the object being pointed to.

The Dialog Box links

The Dialog box is yet another helpful tool. A few words in the dialog box are bright blue and are hyperlinked to the Elements Help page.

Saving Files With Purpose

Now, we want to learn how to use Adobe Photoshop Element to save any file. We shall examine two commands for saving data here.

- ✦ The Save command
- ✦ The Save as command

The Save Command

When you wish to save the changes made to the file that is being worked on, you use the **Save command**. All you have to do to do this is;

- ↕ Select **File** and click on **Save** or use **(Ctrl+S)**

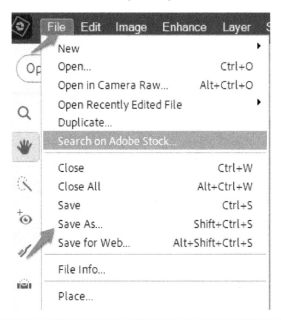

The Save as Command

When saving photos, the Save As command can be used to specify settings such as the file name, file type, layers, etc.

To save files using the **Save As Command**

- ❖ Launch the Photoshop Element and select the image you desire to save as a file
- ❖ Open the **File menu** and click on **Save As**

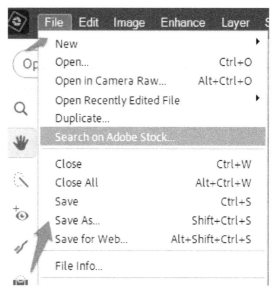

- Select the directory you wish to save the file and enter the name in the Save As text box.
- Click on the **File Format** and select the format you want the file to be saved as (JPEG, GIF, PNG, etc.)
- Then click on **Save**

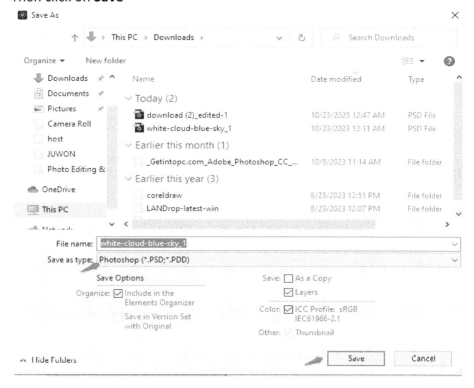

The following list of additional functionalities that some file-saving choices may offer when using the Save As command.

- ✥ **Include In The Element Organizer:** By selecting this option, the saved file is added to the library and made available for viewing in the Photo Browser. However, several file formats, including the EPS file format, do not support the Element organizer.
- ✥ **Save In Version Set With Original**: To keep the various versions of the image organized, this option saves the file and then adds it to a version set in the Photo Browser. You can only access this option if you choose **Include In the Organizer**.
- ✥ **Layer**: The layers in the image are better preserved using this option. When the Layer option is disabled or unavailable, it indicates that there are no layers in the image. A warning icon appears in the Layer check box when the layer in the image needs to be flattened or merged for the chosen format. Choose a different format if you want to keep the layers in an image.
- ✥ **As A Copy:** With the selected option, a duplicate of the open file is saved. The open file's folder receives the file copy after it is saved there.
- ✥ **ICC Profile:** As a result, you can add a color profile to the image for some formats.
- ✥ **Thumbnail:** This option stores the file's thumbnail information. When the Preferences dialog box's Ask When Saving option for Image Preview is activated, this choice is available.
- ✥ **Use Lower Case Extension:** This setting allows either lowercase or uppercase to be used for the file extension.

Saving Files In Different File Formats

To save files in the Adobe Photoshop Element, there are various file types. Here, let's have a look at the file types that Adobe Element supports for file saving.

- ✥ **JPEG (Joint Photographic Expert Group):** Photographs are saved in this file format. This file format selectively removes data to reduce file size while maintaining all of the image's color information. Lower compression results in higher image quality with a bigger file size, whereas higher compression results in lower image quality with a smaller file size. JPEG is the preferred format for displaying or exhibiting images on websites.

- **TIFF (Tagged Image File Format):** This file format, which is a versatile bitmap image format supported by paint, image editing, and page layout programs, is used to transfer files between programs and computer platforms. Most desktop scanners can create TIFF files.

- **PNG (Portable Network Graphics):** On the internet, this is the most used uncompressed raster picture format. Additionally, it is widely used to store digital photos, site designs, and pictures with translucent backgrounds. The Graphics Interchange Format was replaced by the PNG file format (GIF). The PNG picture can exhibit a translucent background, much as the GIF image can. Images in grayscale and 24-bit RGB color palettes can both be found in PNG files.

- **Photoshop (PSD):** This is Photoshop Elements' default file format. With this file format, you can alter an image while maintaining its layers, data, and size.

- **BMP (Bitmap):** To save bitmap digital images regardless of viewing systems, Microsoft Corporation developed this standard image format for MS Windows and OS/2. Uncompressed files, such as those in the BMP file format, are simpler to read. Additionally, the BMP picture file type is no longer supported.

- **CompuServe GIF (Graphics Interchange Format):** Small animations and pictures are regularly shown or shown on web pages using the GIF format. This compressed file format was developed to make files smaller and save time. Only photos in 8-bit color are supported. Use the **Save As Web** command to save an image as a GIF file.

- **Photo Creation Format(PSE):** The typical file format for creating numerous pages is likewise this one. You can save your work in this file format and keep all of your image data and layer information in a multi-page file.

- **Photoshop PDF (Portable Document Format):** The font, page layouts and both vector and bitmap graphics are shown and preserved in this cross-platform and cross-application file format.

- **Pixar:** Pixar image computers may exchange files in this file format. The Pixar workstations were developed and produced for advanced graphics applications, such as those used for 3D animation and three-dimensional imagery. Additionally, this format supports grayscale and RGB.

Saving A File In JPEG Format

To save your file in JPEG format, all that you need to do is:

- ✦ Go to the **File menu** and click on **Save As**

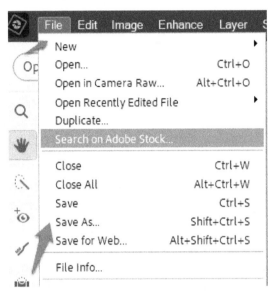

- ✦ Select the folder location you desire to save the file and enter the name in the Save As text box.
- ✦ In the **File format**, Select **JPEG**
- ✦ Then click on **Save**

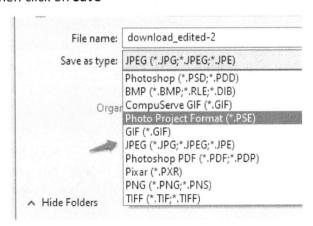

- ✦ The **JPEG dialog box** will appear on this page and when it does
- ✦ Select a **Matte Color** to kindle the appearance of the background opacity, if the image file contains transparency.
- ✦ Identify the image compression and resolution by selecting from the **Quality menu**. To pick the quality level of your image, enter a value between the range of 1 and 12 or drag the **Quality Slider.**
- ✦ Pick **Baseline ("standard"), Baseline Optimized**, or **Progressive** from the **Quality Menu**.
- ✦ Then click on **Ok**

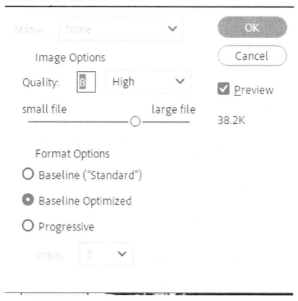

Saving A File In Photoshop PDF Format

Follow the step-by-step guide to save your file in Photoshop PDF format,

Go to the File menu and click on Save As

- ✦ Select the folder location you desire to save the file and enter the name in the Save As text box.

- ✦ In the **File format**, Select **Photoshop PDF**
- ✦ Then click on **Save**

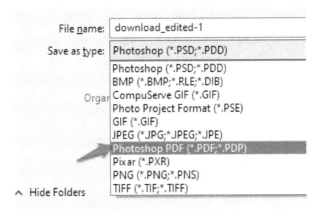

Saving A File In PNG Format

Follow the step-by-step guide to save your file in PNG format,

- ✦ From the File menu click on Save As

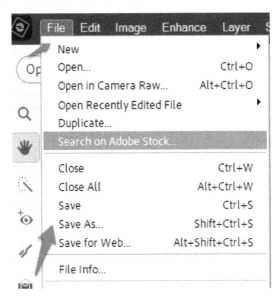

- ✦ Select the folder location you desire to save the file and enter the name in the Save As text box.
- ✦ In the **File format**, Select **Photoshop PDF**
- ✦ Then click on **Save**

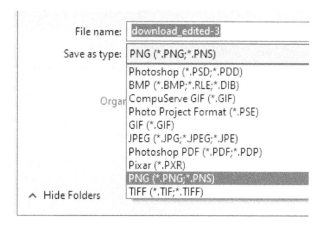

♦ Here on this page, the **PNG dialog box** will open, and when it does
♦ Click on the **Interlace option** to either select **None** or **Interlaced**
- o *None:* The None option displays the image in a browser when the download process is complete
- o **Interlaced**: The Interlay option displays the low resolution of the image downloaded in the browser, making the download time short, but increases the size of the file
♦ Then click on **Ok**

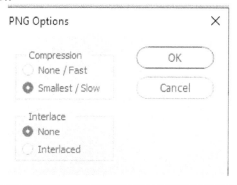

Saving File In GIF format

Follow the step-by-step guide to save your file in **GIF format**

♦ Go to the File Menu and click on Save As

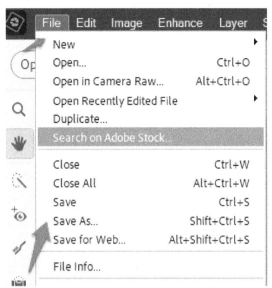

- Select the folder location you desire to save the file and enter the name in the Save As text box.
- In the **File format**, Select **GIF format**
- Then click on **Save**

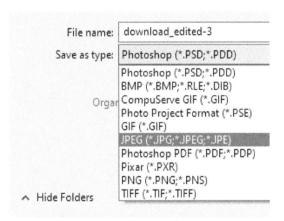

- In the GIF option dialog box, indicate the options you want and then click on **Ok**

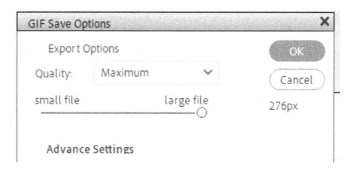

Saving A File In TIFF Format

Follow the step-by-step guide to save your file in TIFF format

✤ Go to the **File menu** and click on **Save As**

✤ Select the folder location you desire to save the file and enter the name in the Save As text box.

✤ In the **File format**, Select **TIFF format**

✤ Then click on **Save**

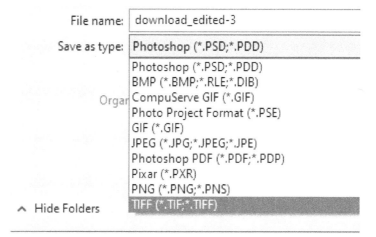

✤ Then **the TIFF Options** dialog box opens where you select the options; the options are listed below

- ○ **Image Compression**: This option is used for indicating or selecting the method for compressing the image data
- ○ **Pixel Order**: This option allows you to choose Interleaved to add the photo to the Element organizer.
- ○ **Byte Order**: This option selects the platform on which the file will be read, especially when you don't know the exact program the file may be opened in

- o **Save Image Pyramid**: This is the option in Adobe Element that preserves multiresolution information. This option allows the image to open at the highest resolution within the file.
- o **Save Transparency**: This is the option that preserves transparency in a file when it is opened in another application.
- o **Layer Compression**: This is the option that specifies or indicates the method for compressing data for pixels in layers. Files with layers are larger than the ones without layers, therefore, compressing the layer reduces the file size.

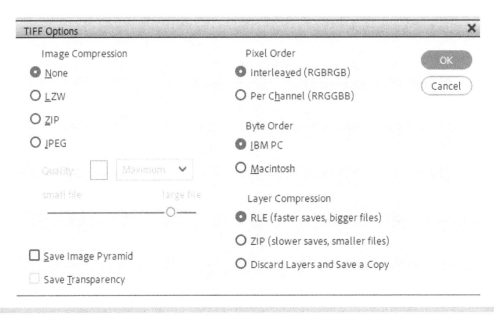

Saving A File In BMP Format

Follow the step-by-step guide to save your file in BIMP Format.

- ✦ Go to the **File menu** and click on **Save As**
- ✦ Select the location you wish to save the file and enter the name in the Save As text box
- ✦ Go to the **File Format** and select the **BMP format**
- ✦ Then click on **Save**

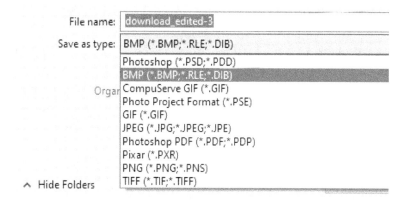

* In the **BMP Options** dialog box, select the file format, indicate the bit depth, and select the **Flip Row Order**. To see other options, click on **Advanced Modes.**
* Click on **OK.**

File Format Compression

Multiple image file formats are used to compress picture data when files are saved in different formats. The two types of file compression are lossy and lossless. Lossless compression preserves all picture data while removing certain features, while lossy compression

The following are the commonly used compression techniques or formats:

- ❖ **RLE (Run Length Encoding)**: This is a lossless compression technique for transparent regions of layers in an image with numerous layers.
- ❖ **LZW (Lemple-Zif-Welch)**: This is a lossless compression algorithm that is mostly used to compress photos with huge sections of only one color.
- ❖ **JPEG**: This is a lossy compression method that works well for compressing photos.
- ❖ **CCIT**: Another lossless compression technique for black-and-white photos is CCIT.
- ❖ **ZIP:** This is another lossless compression technique for images with a wide region of a single color.

Saving Files for The Web

The Save For Web tool is used to compress photos and adjust display parameters so that images may be fine-tuned for usage on web-based media (the Internet), such as blogs and webpages. Before uploading any image to the internet, the file size must be considered, i.e., the file size must be modest to allow for a simple download without compromising the image's quality.

On the web, however, three primary file formats are used: GIF, JPEG, and PNG.

To save files for the web, follow the steps below

- Go to the **File menu** and click on **Save For Web**

- Here, the **Save For Web** dialog box displays a lot of options, and they are listed below
    - ○ **Hand Tool**: When you're zoomed in on the Preview area, you may use this to move about the picture in the Preview area.
    - ○ **Zoom Tool**: This is a tool for enlarging or contracting the preview image.
    - ○ **Eyedropper Tool**: This tool is used to sample a color in an image exactly as it appears in the Preview area. This displays a preview of how the image will appear.
    - ○ **Previews:** once it has been saved. The actual image is shown in the first image, while the preview is shown in the second image.
    - ○ **Preset:** This option allows you to choose from a variety of presets accessible in the drop-down menu. The preset is used to create pre-configured settings for the dialog box's choices.
    - ○ **Image Format**: This is where you choose a file format (GIF, JPEG, or PNG) from the file format drop-down menu.
    - ○ **Quality Settings**: This is where you choose the image's quality before saving it. The Quality choice appears when saving any file as a JPEG; for GIF and PNG, you may specify the color number.
    - ○ **Image Attributes**: The Original Size field in this choice shows the original width and height. In the New Size Area, you may change the image's width and height in pixels or percentages.
    - ○ **Animation**: This option is only available for animated GIFs.
    - ○ **Preview Menu**: This is where you'll find a preview of the output.

CHAPTER THREE

BASIC IMAGE-EDITING CONCEPTS

Working With Pixels

Understanding pixels is necessary before you can effectively manipulate photographs in Photoshop Element.

The basic building blocks of all digital images are pixels. These minute components serve as the foundation for all digital images. The word "picture element" is short for "pixel."

When viewing a photo at a standard zoom level (100 percent or less), the pixels are typically too small to notice, but when we zoom in closer, we notice a lot of tiny squares. A zoomed-in version of the image with visible pixels is shown below.

To get the overall amount of pixels in a photograph, multiply the width and height figures by one another. As an illustration, 300 times 239 equals 71,700.

NOTE: The pixels in an image define the resolution and size of the image.

Understanding Resolution

Element's Image resolution governs or determines how large or tiny an image will be reproduced based on its present size.

The picture resolution is measured in pixels per inch and is determined by the number of pixels in an image file (PPI). The picture resolution will be 200 PPI if there are 200 pixels in a 1-inch horizontal line

The image resolution is important in performing the following

- **Printing Images:** The recommended print resolution is 300 PPI. When the image resolution is too high, the printer takes too long to process the data provided to it, and when the image resolution is too low, the picture quality printed out is poor.
- **Showing Image Screen**: Displaying Picture Screen: The image resolution is determined by the monitor being utilized.

Understanding Image Dimension

The picture dimension refers to the image's width and height. The measurement type for the picture dimension is Pixels by default, but it may also be presented in other units such as **Inches, Percentages, Centimeters, Millimeters, Points**, and **Picas**.

Put on View the Image Resolution and Dimension

The Image Size dialog box is the best place to see the image resolution and dimensions. The Image Size dialog box is also where you may change the size of an image.

There are four aspects of the picture that you may adjust in the Image Size dialog box.

- **Pixel Dimension:** This refers to the image's width and height.
- **Image Size:** This is the value displayed at the top of the dialog box, indicating the image's size.
- **Document Size:** This refers to the image's physical size when printed.
- **Image Resolution When Printed:** This is the number of pixels per inch that appears on the printed image.

To display the Image Size dialog box, follow the steps below

- Go to the **Image Menu** and click on **Resize**
- Then, click on **Image Size** afterward.

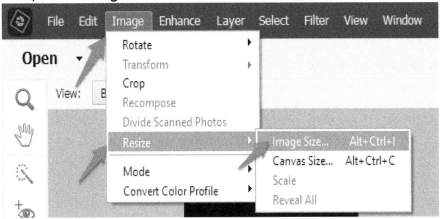

- Here on this page, The **Image Size** dialog box displays the options to change the settings.

An image`s size, resolution, and pixel measurements are determined by the Photoshop Element as follows:

- **Physical Size =**Resolution x pixel dimensions
- **Resolution** = Physical size/pixel dimensions
- **Pixel Dimensions** = Physical Size/Resolution

Resampling Techniques

Resampling is the process of increasing or decreasing the size of a file by adding or subtracting pixels. When you downsample, the number of pixels is reduced, and when you upsample, the number of pixels is increased.

It's worth noting that the quality of the photographs degrades with each resample. You can scan or produce a picture at a reasonably high resolution to prevent resampling.

How to Resample An Image

To effectively resample an image, follow the steps below:

- ✦ Go to the **Image Menu** and click on **Image Size**.

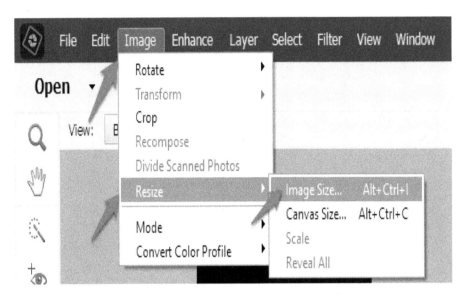

- ✦ In the **Image Size** dialog box, click on the **Resample Image** check box and then select any of the resampling methods.
  - o Nearest Neighbor: This is a resampling approach that is utilized when you have a large number of files with the same color and want to combine them into a smaller file. This procedure is the quickest of them all.
  - o Bilinear: This approach generates a medium-quality image and is suitable for grayscale and line art.
  - o Bicubic: This is the default resampling approach, and it produces decent results.
  - o Bicubic Smoother: This approach is an upgrade on the Bicubic method, with the edges softened slightly. When you wish to upsample a picture, this is the method to utilize.
  - o Bicubic Sharper: This approach creates a high-quality image and outcome and is best employed when downsampling an image.

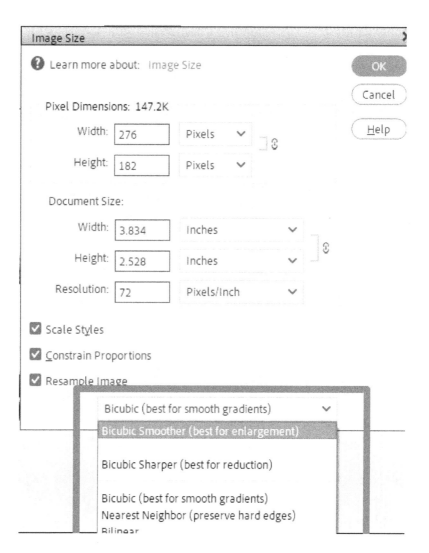

- To apply a variety of style effects to the image, you can click on the **Scale Styles** checkbox in the **Image Size** dialog box
- To maintain the current aspect ratio, click on the **Constraint Proportions** checkbox
- Finally, select the **Ok** button

Selecting a Print or Onscreen Resolution

It's critical to choose the proper resolution for your image before printing or displaying it. This is to guarantee that the image quality is good.

The display resolution is measured in pixels per inch, whereas the printer resolution is measured in ink dots per inch (dpi) (PPI)

The following are the suggested print and onscreen resolutions for a variety of output devices

Output Devices	Optimum Resolution	Acceptable Resolution
Desktop color inkjet and laser printers	300 PPI	180 PPI
Large-format inkjet printer	150 PPI	120 PPI
Professional photo lab printer	300 PPI	200 PPI
Desktop laser printer (Black and white)	170 PPI	100 PPI
Magazine quality (offset press)	300 PPI	225 PPI
Screen image (web, slide show, video)	72 PPI	72 PPI
Tablet devices and smartphones	150 + PPI	150 PPI

Getting Familiar and Proficient with the Use of Color

To learn how to use color in Adobe Photoshop Elements, you must first grasp what RGB (Red, Green, and Blue) is and how it works.

The RGB colors, often known as the additive primaries, are the major or primary colors used in Element. Lighting, video, and displays all employ these hues. The color channels are made up of RGB colors.

The color information for a given channel is kept in the color channels. On a scale of 0 to 255, the red channel stores information about the red color, the green channel stores information about the green color, and the blue channel stores information about the green color. In the red channel, for example, the region that seems whiter or brighter has a more red color, whereas the darker part contains less.

To see the color channels, do the following

- Go to **Enhance Menu** and select **Adjust Lighting**
- Click on **Levels** and the **Levels** dialog box

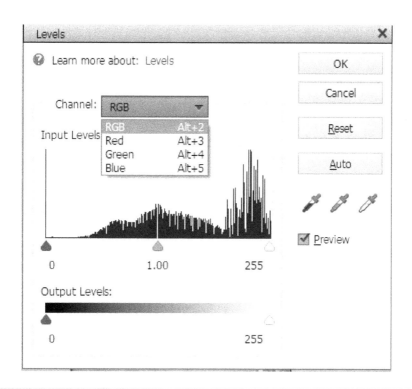

Calibrating Your Monitor

How does it feel to spend hours perfecting an image only to print it out or see it displayed on another device and find that the colors are off?

Hmmm, this is what brings us to calibrating your monitor.

Monitor calibration is the process of measuring and adjusting the colors on your computer monitor to match a common standard.

Failure to calibrate your monitor may prevent you from seeing colors correctly on your screen, which may cause problems with how images appear on other devices or when printed. One proof to know that your monitor needs calibrating is that your image will have an overall color cast, revealing to be washed, or flat when displayed on other devices.

To calibrate your monitor, you will need to use a device called Spectrotometer which works through computer software to maintain the image color.

How to Calibrate a Monitor?

There are several methods for calibrating the monitor, however, using a spectrometer is the most effective and accurate. This device is hung on the screen and is used in conjunction with computer software to measure colors, brightness, contrast, and gamma before developing and storing an ICC (International Color Consortium) profile based on those measurements.

Follow the instructions below to calibrate your monitor
- Allow at least 20-30 minutes for the monitor to warm up before using it, and ensure sure there is no direct light (daylight or ambient light) on it.
- Connect the spectrometer to the computer through a USB connection and position it on top of the screen.
- Follow the software's on-screen directions and wait for it to finish.

NOTE: All types of grayscales and colors will show on the screen when using the spectrometer to calibrate the monitor, and the spectrometer will record them and utilize them to create an ICC profile that is stored on the computer.

Selecting A Color Scheme For Your Workspace

After calibrating the display, the color workspace, which can be either sRGB or Adobe RSG, must be set. Follow the steps below to access the color workplace settings.

- Go to the **Edit** menu and select **Color Settings** from the drop-down menu

✦ Select any of the choices in the **Color Settings** dialog box, as illustrated in the figure below.

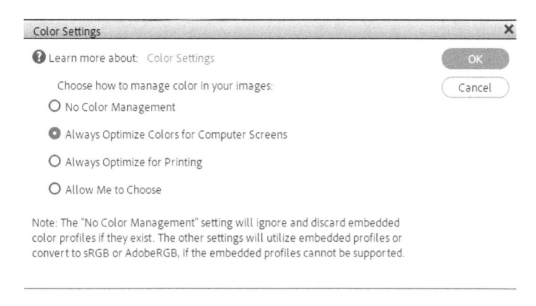

The following describes each choice in the Color Settings dialog box.

✦ • **No Color Management:** When this option is selected, all color management is disabled and the display profile is used as the working space. When opening photos, this option eliminates any embedded profiles and does not tag when saving.

✦ • **Always Optimize Colors For Computer Screen:** When this option is chosen, the workspace is adjusted to sRGB using the ratio button. The sRGB color space is ideal for seeing images on a monitor and printing.

✦ • **Always Optimize For Printing:** This option lets you set your workspace to Adobe RGB (1998), which retains embedded profiles and assigns Adobe RGB to untagged files when you open them. New monitors and inkjet printers perform well in this environment because of the color. It is set to this option by default

✦ **Allow Me To Choose:** This option allows you to select sRGB or Adobe RGB when opening untagged files.

Understanding the functions of profile

For accurate and consistent color management, every color device in your system must have an exact ICC-compliant profile. For example, the image displayed on the monitor could appear different in the absence of a particular monitor profile. To prevent misleading depiction, which costs time and effort, this requires a detailed profile.

The different kinds of profiles we have are:

- **Monitor Profiles:** The monitor profile should be the first one you create because it enables you to see color accurately on the display. This helps explain how the monitor is now showing a color.
- **Input Device Profile:** The input device profile specifies the color that the input device can record or scan. When a profile selection is possible when using a digital camera, Adobe advises using Adobe RGB or sRGB (the default option).
- **Output Device Profile:** The color space that output devices like desktop printers and printing presses use is specified here. The color management system uses the output device to map the colors in a document to the colors in the output device's color space. The output profile should take into account any particular printing considerations, such as the type of paper and ink.
- **Document Profiles:** This details the precise RGB or CMYK color space for the page. The program shows a description of the document's true color appearance when you assign or tag a document with a profile. When Color Management is enabled, Adobe programs use the Working Space choices made in the Color Settings dialog box to determine which profile to apply to a new document. Untagged documents only have a raw color number and no profile has been assigned to them. When working with untagged documents, the Adobe program utilizes the current working space profile to display and modify colors.

CHAPTER FOUR

CHECKING OUT THE PHOTO EDITOR

This chapter will take us to the Photo Editor in the Advanced Edit mode, building on our discussion of the Photo Editor in the Quick Edit mode in Chapter 2 of this book. Before we get started with this chapter, it is pertinent to know that Expert Edit mode has been changed to Advanced Edit mode, and this will be displayed for you to see as we begin to tour around the Photo Editor in the Advanced Edit mode.

Going Deeper Into Photo Editor In the Advanced Edit Mode

The screen's image is what you see when you first enter Advanced Edit mode. Some of the tools will be familiar to you if you're used to working in a Windows environment. You must first become familiar with the many tools, panels, and other objects in the environment by learning their names and positions. Then you start to pick up using the many tools, panels, and other things around you.

The following features are available when you open the Photo Editor in Expert Mode.

- ✦ **The System Menu Button:** On the left side of the menu bar, this is accessible. Simply click the button to use this feature, then select an option from the list that appears.

♦ **The Menu Bar:** Task-execution commands are provided in this section. The menu bar's commands include **File, Edit, Image, Enhance, Layer, Select, Filter, View**, and **Help**. The shortcut keys are located in the menu bar to the right of the various subcommands.

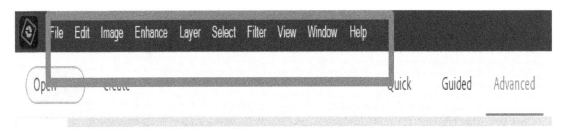

♦ **The Open Bar:** This may be found underneath the menu bar on the left-hand side of the status bar. The Open option at the far left end of the shortcuts bar may be used to open previously opened photos as well as create new files.

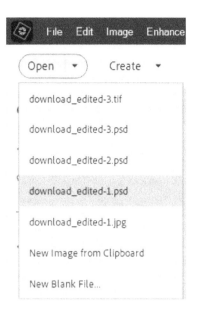

* **The Edit Buttons:** In the Photo Editor, these buttons are the very center of the shortcut bar. They enable you to choose between **Quick, Guided,** and **Advanced** modes.

* **The Share**: This is located on the far right side of the Home screen. You may use this button to make and share calendars, collages, and more.

* **The Create Button:** This button is located beside the Open bar. This is used to create content such as Slide show, Photo Collage, Photo Reels, Quote graphics, etc.

- **Status Bar:** It is the bar that gives you insight into the picture you`re working on at the moment.

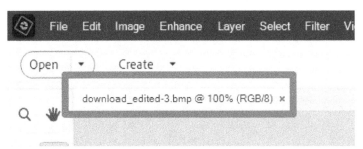

- **The Tool Box/Panel:** This selection offers the tools for editing photos in the Photo Editor. A few of the tools that are offered include the Zoom Tool, Hand Tool, Move Tool, Lasso Tool, Quick Selection, Spot Healing, Clone Stamp, Eraser, Gradients, Red Eye, Smart Brush, Blur, Paint Bucker, Color Picker, Horizontal Type, and others. This option is located on the left-hand side of the Home screen.

- **The Tool Options And Photo Bin:** They may be found beneath the Status bar. The Tool Options menu lets you customize the options for the different tools in the Toolbox. You may see or open photographs in the Photo Bin by pressing the Photo Bin Button. Click the Photo Bin button at the bottom left of the window to move to the Photo Bin, and the same goes for the Tool Options.

- **The Image Window:** This is the Photoshop Element program's primary workspace. The numerous photos that are opened and made are displayed in the image window at the very top.

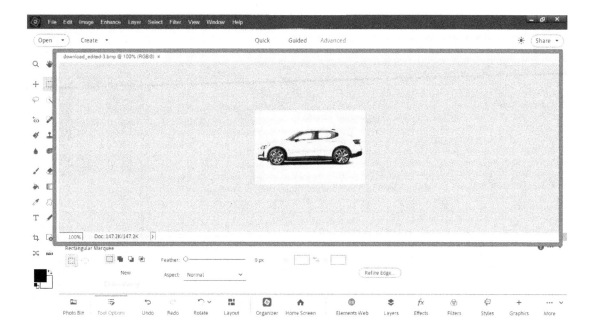

❖ **Photo Tabs:** Unlike the status bar that only displays information about a current tab, The Photo Tab contains all of the photographs that have been opened in the Photo Editor, and they are displayed by default in several tabs at the top of the window.

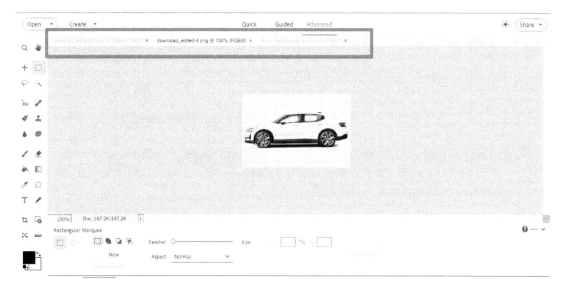

❖ **Panel Bin:** The Layer panels are seen in this. Click on the symbol at the Panel Bin's bottom to change the panel. The Layers panel, Effect panel, Graphics panel, and Favorites panel are all included in the Panel Bin.

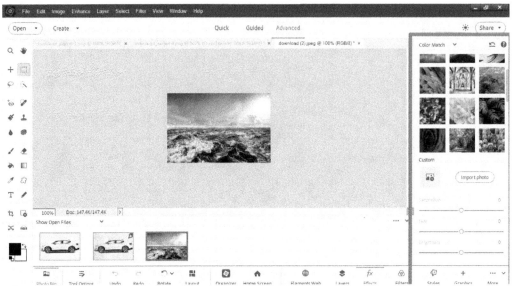

❖ **Undo/Redo:** These are highly significant commands in the Photo Editor, and they are situated next to the Photo Bin/Tool Options.

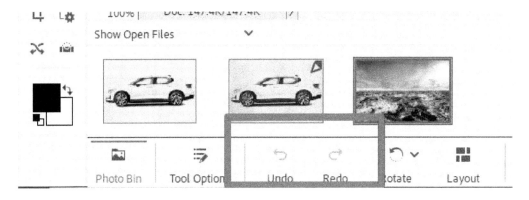

❖ **Rotate:** When you select this option, a menu appears, allowing you to choose whether to rotate the picture in the Image Window using the Clockwise or Counterclockwise tool.

61

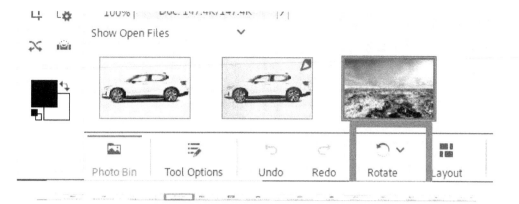

✦ **Layout:** This feature in the Photo Editor permits you to decide how your image files will appear, either in rows, columns, or as a grid in the image window.

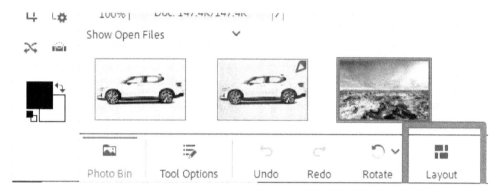

✦ **Organizer:** The Organizer may be found on the Home Screen's right side. To maintain an effective and organized image collection, use this to import, view, and arrange pictures. Features for categorizing, ranking, sorting, and locating your photographs are available in the Organizer.

✦ **Home Screen:** This feature permits its user to open the home screen of the Photoshop Element.

- **Elements Web:** This option allows you access to the official site of Adobe Elements.

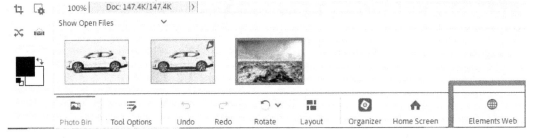

- **Photo Bin Options Menu:** When you click on this button, a pop-up menu of options appears, including printing chosen images and creating a creation from photos picked in the Photo Bin.

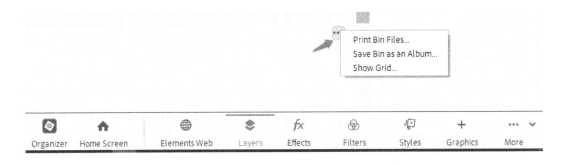

Opening The Image Window

This is the Photoshop Element program's primary workspace. The numerous pictures that are opened and made are displayed in the Image Window's window at the very top. When you open a picture in the Image Windows, you get access to numerous sophisticated tools and capabilities.

To open an image in an Image Window, follow the steps below

✦ Go to **File** and choose **Open**

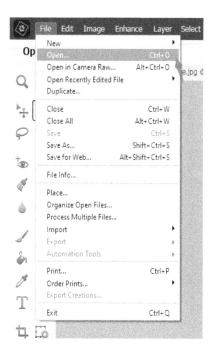

✦ The Open dialog box will now display, allowing you to browse the folder and choose the desired photographs.
✦ Select the desired picture, and then click the **Open** button.

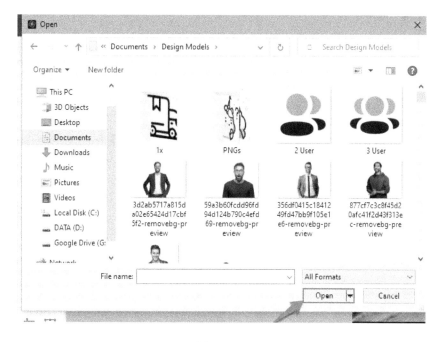

The following are the important items that will be displayed in the Image Window

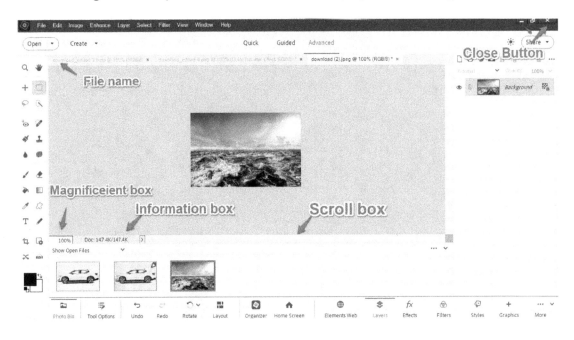

✦ **File Name:** Each file that is opened in the image window has its filename shown. The filename appears above the image window in the Photo Editor.

✦ **Close Button:** The X symbol to the left of the filename denotes the Close button, which closes the file.

✦ **Scroll Bars:** When you zoom closer on an image, the Scroll bar becomes active. You may use the scroll arrows, the scroll bar, or the Hand tool in the Tools pane to move the picture within the win

✦ **Magnificent Box:** This option allows you to view how a picture is zoomed in or out at a glance.

✦ **Information Box:** This option allows you to choose the information to be displayed by choosing out of options from the pop-up menu.

   ✦ **Sizing The Window:** To resize the window, drag any corner in or out when the image is undocked and not viewed as a tab.

Now that we've covered the Image Window in greater depth, let's move on to the Information Box's pop menu.

   ✦ **Document Sizes:** This option displays details about the stored files' size and resolution.

- **Document Profile:** This option shows you the file's color profile.
- **Document Dimension:** This displays the physical size of the document in your preferred measurement unit, such as inches.
- **Current Selected Layer:** You may pick Current Selected Layer as a readout by clicking on a layer in the Layer panel and selecting it.
- **Scratch Sizes:** This option shows how much Memory each open document takes up.
- **Efficiency:** In comparison to utilizing the scratch disk, this defines how many operations are performed. The RAM is consumed when the number reaches 100%. When the percentage goes below 100%, the scratch disk is used.
- **Timing:** This indicates how long it took to complete the preceding operation.
- **Current Tool:** This is where the name of the tool chosen from the Touch panel is shown.

Recognizing Contextual Menus

Most apps use contextual menus as standard commands; Photoshop Element does the same, especially in the Photo Editor and Organizer. Commands pertinent to the tool, selection, or panel that is now selected are displayed in the contextual menu.

When the contextual menu is engaged, the menu commands vary based on the features and tools you are using as well as where you are clicking. This is because the contextual menu offers guidance according to the objects, tools, and area you are clicking. The contextual menu can be accessed by doing the following

- Place the pointer over an image or a panel item.
- Right-click and pick or select a command from the menu.

NOTE:

- You may access the contextual menu from the Menu bar
- The context menu is missing from several panel objects

Selecting The Tools

Before learning how to select tools in the Tools Panel, let's familiarize ourselves with the various tools there, especially in the Advanced Edit Mode.

The Toolbox In The Quick Mode

The toolbox in Quick mode has a few sets of tools that can be used rapidly. The accessible tools include Zoom, Hand, Quick Selection, Eye, Whiten Teeth, Straighten, Type, Spot Healing Brush, Crop, and Move.

During the course of studying the tools in Expert Mode, we will be listing out their functions.

The Toolbox In The Advanced Mode

The toolbox in the Advanced mode is more advanced and potent than the toolbox in the Quick mode. The toolbox in Expert mode will be divided into the following categories.

- View
- Select
- Enhance
- Draw
- Modify

Tool In The View Group Of The Advanced Mode Toolbox

TOOLS	BUTTON	USES

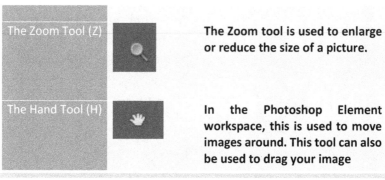

The Zoom Tool (Z)		The Zoom tool is used to enlarge or reduce the size of a picture.
The Hand Tool (H)		In the Photoshop Element workspace, this is used to move images around. This tool can also be used to drag your image

Tools In The Select Group Of The Advanced Mode

TOOLS	BUTTONS	USES
The Move Tool (V)		This is used to move layers and selections inside Photoshop Element.
The Rectangular Marquee Tool (M)		This is used to draw a rectangular box around an area in the picture. Hold the Shift key to make the selection a square.
The Elliptical Marquee Tool (M)		This is used to create an elliptical selection. Hold the Shift key to make the selection a circle.
The Lasso Tool (L)		This allows you to draw a free-form selection in a section of the image.
The Magnetic Lasso Tool (L)		When a shape in a picture is chosen, this tool helps to create a high contrast high-contrast N outline
olygonal Tool (L)		This is used to create selection border segments with straight edges.
The Quick Selection Tool		This tool produces a color and texture selection on

		any part of the picture that is selected or dragged.
The Selection Brush Tool (A)	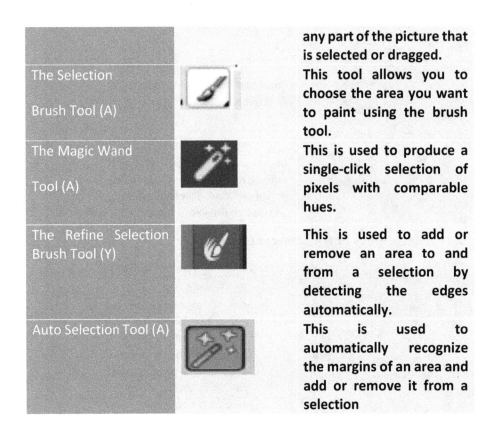	This tool allows you to choose the area you want to paint using the brush tool.
The Magic Wand Tool (A)		This is used to produce a single-click selection of pixels with comparable hues.
The Refine Selection Brush Tool (Y)		This is used to add or remove an area to and from a selection by detecting the edges automatically.
Auto Selection Tool (A)		This is used to automatically recognize the margins of an area and add or remove it from a selection

Tools In The Enhance Group Of The Advanced Mode Toolbox

TOOLS	BUTTON	USES
The Eye Tool		This eliminates the red-eye effect, and the pet-eye appearance, and corrects closed eyelids in your photos.
The Spot Healing Brush (J)		This is used to erase a blemish from a picture by choosing a portion of the image.
The Smart Brush Tool (F)		This is the tool that adjusts the tone and color balance of particular regions of a picture.

The Detail Smart Brush Tool (F)		This tool, like the painting tool, allows you to paint particular sections of a photo with adjustments.
The Clone Stamp Tool (S)		This tool uses an image sample to paint over things in your image, which may be used to replicate objects, eliminate image imperfections, or paint over objects.
The Pattern Stamp Tool (S)		This tool is used to create a pattern on top of a picture.
The Blur Tool (R)		This is used to soften the rough edges or regions by removing some edges.
The Sharpen Tool (R)		This tool sharpens a picture by concentrating on the image's soft edges to improve clarity and focus.
The Smudge Tool (R)		The tool aids in the stimulation of a wet paint-smearing brush. This tool takes the color from where the stroke begins and moves it to the location where you drag it.
The Sponge Tool (O)		This is used to alter the color saturation of a specific region in a picture.
The Dodge Tool (O)		This is used to make portions of a picture lighter. This tool may also be used to bring out features in shadows.
The Burn Tool (O)		This is the tool used to darken areas of an image. Also, this tool can be used to bring out details in the highlight

Tools In The Draw Group Of The Advanced Mode

TOOLS	BUTTON	USES
The Brush Tool (B)		This is used to make color strokes that are soft or harsh. It may also be used to improve retouching skills.
The Impressionist Brush Tool (B)		This is used to make adjustments to the image's color and details.
The Color Replacement Tool(B)G		This tool reduces the number of particular colors in your photo.
The Eraser Tool (E)		As you navigate across the images of the photo, this tool assists in the removal of pixels.
The Background Eraser Tool (E)		This tool is used to convert the color of a pixel to transparent pixels so that an item may be easily removed from its background
Magic Eraser Tool (E)		This is used to change pixels that are similar when dragged within a photo.
Paint Bucket Tool (K)		This is the tool that is used to fill an area with a color value that is comparable to the pixels you select.
Pattern Tool (K)		Instead of utilizing one of the brush tools, you may use this tool to apply a fill or pattern to your picture.
Gradient Tool (G)		This is the tool that creates a gradient in a specific region of an image.
Color Picker Tool (I)		This is the tool that duplicates the color of a section in an image and uses it to create a new backdrop or foreground.

Custom Shape Tool (U)	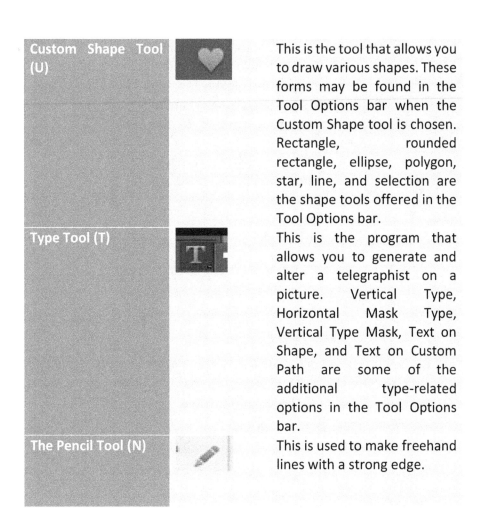	This is the tool that allows you to draw various shapes. These forms may be found in the Tool Options bar when the Custom Shape tool is chosen. Rectangle, rounded rectangle, ellipse, polygon, star, line, and selection are the shape tools offered in the Tool Options bar.
Type Tool (T)		This is the program that allows you to generate and alter a telegraphist on a picture. Vertical Type, Horizontal Mask Type, Vertical Type Mask, Text on Shape, and Text on Custom Path are some of the additional type-related options in the Tool Options bar.
The Pencil Tool (N)		This is used to make freehand lines with a strong edge.

Tools In The Modify Group Of The Advanced Mode Toolbox

TOOLS	BUTTONS	USES
The Crop Tool (C)		This tool allows you to trim the part of a selected image.
The Cookie Cutter Tool (C)		With this tool, you can crop an image to any desired shape.
The Perspective Crop Tool (C)		When cropping a picture, this tool is used to change the viewpoint of the image.

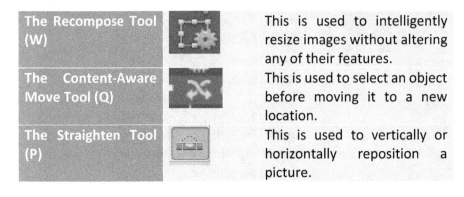

The Recompose Tool (W)		This is used to intelligently resize images without altering any of their features.
The Content-Aware Move Tool (Q)		This is used to select an object before moving it to a new location.
The Straighten Tool (P)		This is used to vertically or horizontally reposition a picture.

All you have to do is adhere to any of the following steps to choose any of the tools described above.

- Select a tool in the toolbox
- To choose any of the tools you want to utilize, use the keyboard shortcut. For example, pressing P will activate the Straighten tool.
- A Shift key can be configured to choose a tool. The preferences settings govern this. If you wish to alter the default settings so that you never again need to press the Shift key, adhere to the instructions below.
  - From the **Edit** menu, go to **Preference**
  - Select **General** and then deselect the **Use Shift** key for the **Tool Switch** check box.

Selecting From The Tool Options

In the Element window, the Tool Options bar is shown at the bottom. Several choices are available in the Tool Options section to be applied to a chosen tool. For instance, the Tool Options menu appears when you click on the Lasso Tool and lists the Polygonal Lasso Tool and Magnetic Lasso Tool.

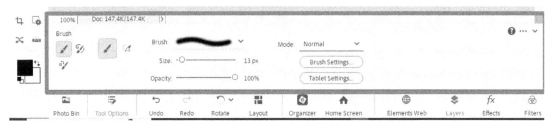

Using The Panels

The panels are on the right-hand side of the main screen, in both Quick and Advanced Edit modes. An Adjustment panel, Effects, Textures, and Frames are all included in the Quick Edit mode. The Advanced edit mode, on the other hand, has a larger range of panels, including Layers, Effects, Filters, Styles, Graphics, and More.

Let's quickly review the panels in both Quick Edit and Expert Edit modes.

- ✦ **Layers**: This is the most important panel out of all the others. The layer panel lets you add features like text, numerous photographs, and other items to different layers in the document when working on a creative project. Using the layer's panel, you can edit any project at any point during the production process. The layer panel's top-left corner has access to several tools, and the top-right corner has an icon with horizontal lines.
- ✦ **Effects:** This section provides menus and tabs for selecting different effects to apply to images. This panel offers the user complex recipes that can be applied to any image with a single click, including automatic color, special effects, and other capabilities.
- ✦ **Graphics:** Clip art, text effects, scalable vector shapes, and a variety of picture frame designs are all available under the Graphics tab and may be applied or added to an image with a single click. You may sort and filter objects in the panel by Type, Activity, Mood, Event, Object, Season, and many other criteria. Some features are also available for download through Adobe's official websites
- ✦ **Filter:** This is a little thumbnail that shows how each FX filter works. Simply click on the thumbnail to activate the effect. There are 98 distinct filters to choose from, each having billions of possible combinations.
- ✦ **Styles:** This is used to alter the image by applying a filter to the entire layer. Drop shadows, glow, bevels, patterns, and glass button effects are all available under the Styles tab. There are 176 different styles in the Styles section.
- ✦ **Textures:** This collection includes a variety of creative elements like sun beams and light leaks that may be used as backgrounds, web pages, and more. With a single click, you may add a textured overlay to your image. You may also use your Adobe account to acquire new textures or overlays.

- **More:** The More panel is positioned to the right of the Graphics panel in the main window's bottom right corner. A pop-up menu appears when you click the More panel, providing you access to extra panels that aren't shown in the Panel bin. Below is a quick explanation of the additional panels.
  - o **Actions:** Element inherited this function from Adobe Photoshop. This feature enables you to automate several adjustments to your photograph. Replaying certain actions or interactions on the images is a feature of this functionality. Additional Actions, like those for cropping, resizing, copying, and adding a border to photos, are also available online for download and integration with the Elements.
  - o **Adjustments:** Sliders for exposure, lighting, color, balance, and sharpness adjustments are available in the adjustment panels.
  - o **Color Swatches:** To select the color type to use, use the Color Swatches panels. This kind of backdrop color can be painted with a paintbrush or a pencil. You can create your custom color Swatch using these panels to complete a certain project.
  - o **Histogram:** When this panel is opened, a variety of tones that can be added or applied to any image in the foreground are displayed. Midtone, highlights, whites, blacks, underexposed, and overexposed are some of these tones.
  - o **Info:** The readout for various color values and the physical dimensions of your photographs are provided or displayed by this panel.
  - o **Navigator:** This feature permits one to zoom in and hover around an image in the image window.
  - o **Custom Workspace:** Panels are docked and undocked here. Additionally, this panel enables you to create a personalized workspace according to your preferences.
- **Create/Share Panel:** The Create panel is used for creations such as calendars, greeting cards, photo books, greeting cards, and lots more. The share panel contains many tools for sharing photos

Working With The Photo Bin

The Photo Bin can be found beneath the Element window and above the taskbar. It can be used for several functions, including opening and closing photos, hiding photos, rotating photos, and viewing file metadata. Any image that has been opened in the Image window is displayed as a thumbnail in the Photo Bin. You can move many open photographs across locations using the Photo Bin.

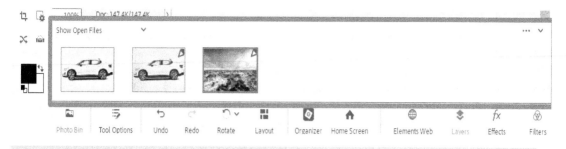

| Photo Bin | Tool Options | Undo | Redo | Rotate | Layout | Organizer | Home Screen | Elements Web | Layers | Effects | Filters |

Displaying Different Views Of The Same Image

Follow these instructions to display the same view of the same image.

- ✦ Select the image's thumbnail in the Photo Bin and go to the **View** menu
- ✦ Select **New Window** for the image name.

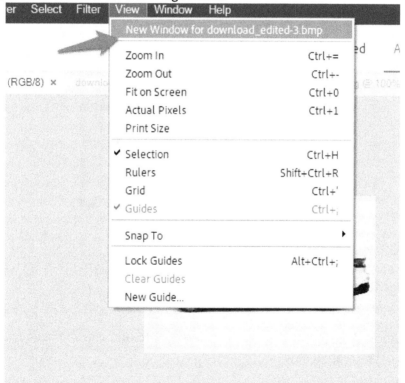

- ✦ A new image is displayed on the Image window and a new thumbnail is added in the Photo Bin
- ✦ To switch to another different view of the same image, double-click on the Thumbnails in the Photo bin.
- ✦ You can also zoom this image by clicking on the Zoom tool in the Tool panels.

Getting Very Familiar With The Photo Bin Actions

There are a few more options for handling the pictures in the Photo Bin under the Photo Bin Actions menu. To access these options, as shown in the picture below, click on the tiny four-line square in the bin's upper right corner.

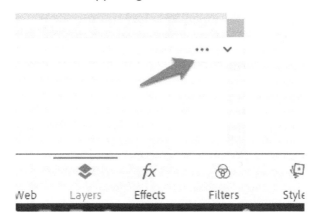

The Photo Bin Actions do the following tasks.

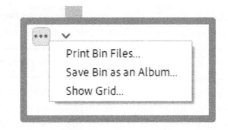

- ◆ **Print Bin Files**: When you want to print any file from the Photo Bin, this option comes in useful. To do so, first, choose the file you want to print, then select Print Bin Files from the drop-down menu. After that, you'll see the Print dialog box, where you may print the photo prints of the selected file.

- ◆ **Save Bin As An Album**: You may use this tool to add extra images to an existing album or to create a new one.

- ◆ **Show Grid:** This is used to create a grid around photos in the Photo bin.

Touring around the Guided Mode

The Photoshop Element's advanced Guided Edit mode allows you to make simple decisions about your photos and leave the rest to the computer.

The purpose of the Guided Edit mode, as its name suggests, is to walk you through a variety of editing activities step-by-step.

Go to the Shortcut bar and select **Guided** to use the Guided Edit mode.

There are six categories of the Guide Edit mode and they are as follows:
- **The Basics Edit**: This edit permits you to make changes to the images via features such as brightness and contrast, correct skin tone, crop photo, levels, and so on.
- **The Color Edit**: This allows you to effect changes to the color of your images using features such as enhanced color, lomo camera effect, removing a cast color, saturated film effect, etc.
- **The Black Edit and White Edit**: As the name implies, this edition allows you to convert all or part of the photo to black and white using features such as B&W color pop, B&W selection, and so on.
- **The Fun Edit**: With the Fun edit, you can apply interesting features to your images using features such as meme maker, double exposure, multi-photo text, etc.
- **The Special Edits**: The Special edit allows you to apply creative and artistic effects to your photos using features such as depth of field, frame creator, Orton effect, perfect landscape, etc.
- **The Photomerge Edit**: The Photomerge Edit allows you to combine or connect multiple images or photos to produce a new image. The Photomerge edit contains features such as Photomerge compose, Photomerge exposure, Photomerge faces, and Photomerge group.

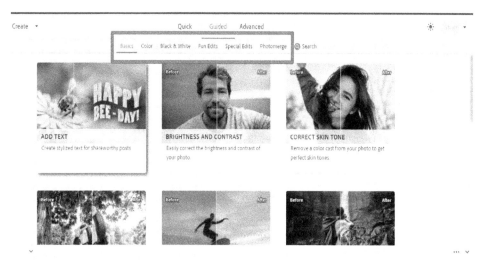

Exploiting The Editing Environment

In the next session of this book, we will discuss the preference settings. By employing preference options, you can adapt a program to your working style and personalize your job.

There are two Preference dialog boxes in Adobe Photoshop Element: one located in the Organizer and one in the Photo Editor. The Preference dialog box in Photo Editor will be the main topic of this lesson.

How to Launch and Navigate Preferences Using the Photo Editor

The Preference dialog box in the Photo Editor separates the options into panes for carrying out various tasks in Photoshop Element. When the Preference dialog box is opened, the General pane is the first to show up.

- ✢ To open the Preference dialog box
- ✢ Go to the **Edit** menu, click on **Preference,** and select **General**
- ✢ Here, the **Preference** dialog box will be displayed.

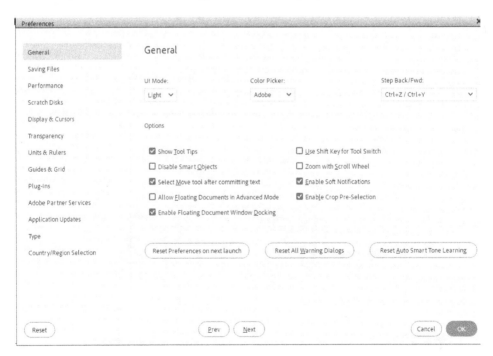

With brevity, let`s take a look at the features in the Preference dialog box and how they function.

- **Panelists**: The Panelist is located at the left-hand side of the Preference dialog box displaying various panels such as General, Saving files, Scratch disks, etc. Clicking on any of these pages automatically opens you to additional options you can work with.
- **Ok**: This is used to confirm any change made in any of the panes and close the Preference dialog box
- **Cancel**: When clicked on, this returns to the same settings as when you first opened a pane, and finally closed the dialog box
- **Reset**: This option returns the Preference dialog box to the same settings as when it was first opened. After resetting, the dialog box stays open, where you set the new settings.
- **Prev**: This is used to move to the previous pane
- **Next**: This is used to move to the next pane.

NOTE: Panes are sections in the Preference dialog box

Studying All of the Preference Panes

There are numerous panes with a variety of functions in the preference panes. Let's examine each pane and its purposes in more detail.

- **General Preference**: This is where you may alter the general settings for the editing environment.
- **Saving Files References**: This refers to the file-saving options offered. You may add extensions to filenames and save files with picture previews, layers, and compatibility choices in this section
- **Performance Preference**: This is the window where you can see the historical statistics as well as the memory settings, which are responsible for assigning memory in Photoshop Element.
- **Scratch Disks**: This is the pane that is responsible for using the hard drive as an extension of the RAM
- **Display & Cursor Preferences**: You may customize how various tool cursors are shown, as well as how the Crop tools are displayed while cropping photographs in these panels.
- **Transparency Preferences**: Here in these panes, you get to select how transparency will be displayed in the Element
- **Units & Ruler Preferences:** This enables you to specify the column guide, ruler units, and document default resolutions.
- **Guides & Grid Preferences**: This provides features for gridline color, divisions, subdivision,

80

- **Plugins Preference**: This is in charge of selecting another Plug-Ins folder. The Plug-Ins are third-party programs that assist you to perform tasks that aren't included in Element. You may find the Photoshop Element Plug-Ins on the internet.
- **Adobe Partner Services:** This enables Elements to look for new services, delete any data stored online, and reset all account information.
- **Application Updates:** These allow you to automatically update the Element application or receive an alert when a new version is ready.
- **Type Preferences:** This is where you can change the text attributes for the setting. You can preview font sizes as well as use font types such as Asian characters that show the font name in English.
- **Country/Region:** This allows you to select a country or region from the drop-down menu.

CHAPTER FIVE

MOVING WITHIN THE ORGANIZER

The Organizer, which is located on the right side of the Home Screen and was previously discussed in this book, is where you import, explore, and arrange photos to keep your image collection effective and organized. The Organizer has tools for categorizing, ranking, sorting, and locating your pictures.

Additionally, you'll discover how to load pictures into this program from CDs, DVDs, scanners, phones, and tablets.

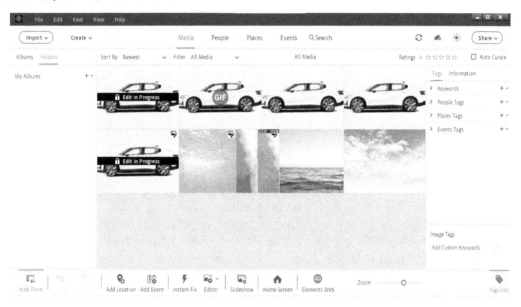

Sorting Images and Media On the Hard Drive

The photos and media occupy the majority of the hard disk. If there are numerous images, they would need to be categorized for reference. Designating a folder is the wisest course of action. Any name you choose, including dates, locations, events, and so on, can be used for the folder. Once you've finished, you may start placing the pictures in folders. The Organizer can be used to import files as well.

Uploading Images to the organizer

Any photograph you want to import into your organizer must first be saved to your computer's hard drive.

The following techniques can be used to upload pictures from a camera or other device to the physical components of your computer.

✦ In the Organizer, go to the **File** menu, click on **Get Photo and Videos,** and then select **From Files and Folder** from the right-hand side

✦ Browse through your hard disk and select the image you wish to add in the **Get Photo and Videos dialog box**

✦ Then click on the **Get Media button**

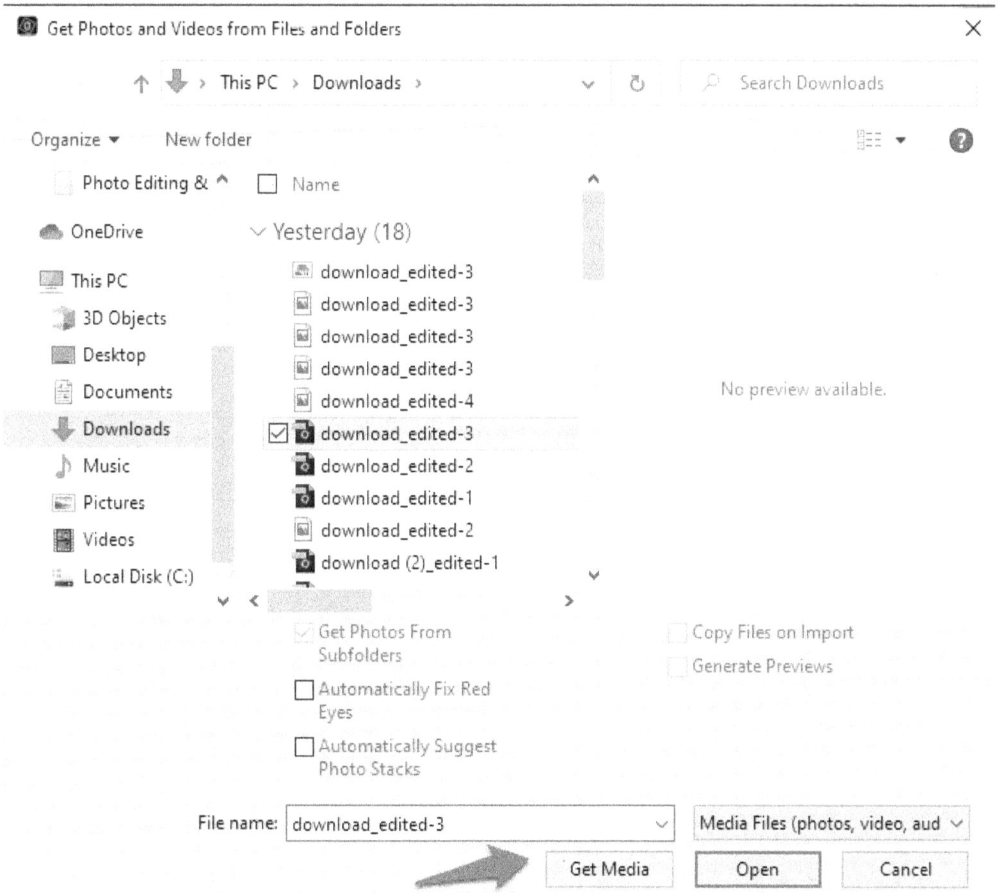

Downloading Camera Images With The Element Downloader

To get images from your camera to your Organizer, follow the procedures below

- Insert the media card from the camera or connect the camera to your computer via a USB port
- Open the **Organizer Window**
- Go to the **File menu,** select **Get Photo and Videos,** and then click on **From Camera or Card Reader.**

- In the **Adobe Photo Downloader** dialog box, go to the **Get Photos From** drop-down list and select the media card
- Select the **Browse** button to find the folder you wish to copy the image from
- Click on the **Get Media** button to import the photos

Working with the Media Browser

Every image or photo imported into the Organizer is shown as thumbnails in the Organizer's center via the Media Browser, which can be found inside the Organizer.

Viewing images from a folder that has been chosen in the Media browser takes place in the Import panel.

As seen below, there is an Import panel with a list of folders on the left side of the Media browser.

- **The list View:** This view lists all of the imported folders in alphabetical order. The files in the subfolder are not organized hierarchically. This is the default view in the Media Browser by default.
- **The Tree View:** In this mode, the photos in the Media Browser are displayed in a hierarchical order. To switch to this view, select View as Tree from the Menu drop-down menu.

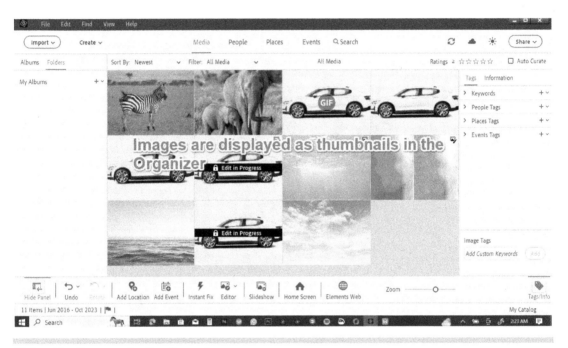

Using the Scanner in the Organizer

Scanner scans of your slides, negatives, and photos can be obtained by using the organizer in Photoshop Element. The scanner can be connected to the card readers and camera using the same USB or FireWire ports.

Image Requirements for Scanning in Photoshop Element

On the scanner device, you can configure the resolution and color settings before you begin scanning. Before scanning a file, you can choose the resolution you desire. Take into account the following elements to help you when scanning.

- ✦ **Grayscale Images**: These are graphics that don't have any color, but instead rely on gradients, such as different shades of black, to create an image. As a result, the grayscale image should be scanned at 600 dpi or above and saved as a PNG file.
- ✦ **Line Art:** This is a type of imagery that comprises solely lines and curves, with no colors or gradients (shadings). Cartoons, comics, ideographs, and glyphs are all examples of line art. Scanning line art at 900 dpi for print and 300 dpi for the web is recommended.
- ✦ **Halftone:** These are visuals made up of tiny dots. Tone mapping photos should be scanned at a DPI of 1200 or above to ensure that the halftone is correctly captured by the scanner.
- ✦ **Color:** Colored images are the most commonly scanned images. Set the scan resolution to 600 dpi for pictures, and 300 dpi for the web, and save in PNG for colorful images.

Using the Scanner to Import Images

Make sure the Scanner software is correctly installed on your computer by adhering to the directions provided in the manual before using your scanner to acquire any photographs. To import photos from your scanner into the Organizer, follow the steps listed below.

- ✦ First, confirm that your scanner is turned on and linked to your computer.
- ✦ Select **Get Photo and Videos** from the **File menu**, then click on **From Scanner**.

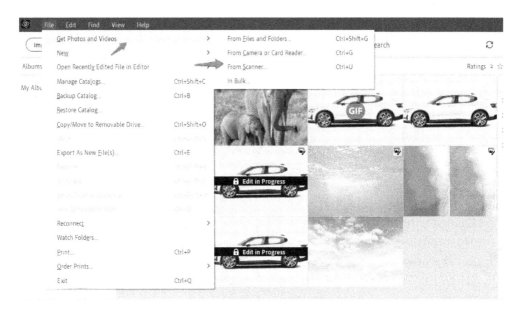

- In the **Get Photos From Scanner** dialog box, select the name of the scanner to use in the **Scanner** drop-down menu
- Click on **Browse** to change the location to save the photos
- Click on **Save** to change the file format of the photos and drag the **Quality slider** to increase or decrease the quality of the scan
- Then click on **Ok.**

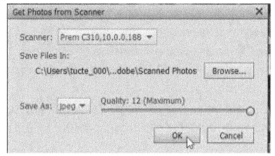

- In the dialog box that pops up, you can make other adjustments to the scanned image, and when you are done, click on the Scan button.

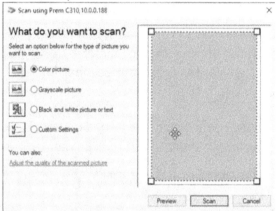

Exporting Images with your Mobile Devices

From a variety of phones, including iPhones, iPods, and other mobile devices, you can transfer media files. To import pictures from your phone into your Organizer, follow the steps below.

- Go to **File,** select **Get Photos and Videos,** and click on **From Files and Folder**
- Navigate through the folder in which you copied the file and then them to the organizer
- Get the device connected with a USB cable
- When the **Photo Downloader** opens, click on the **Browse** button, open the **Select Directory** to **Store Files window**

- Select a destination folder and then click on **Select Folder** to see where the photos are saved
- Click on the **Get Media button** to import the photos into your computer.

Additionally, you may use Apple's iTunes to upload photographs from Element to the iPhone, iPod touch, or iPad. Follow these procedures to accomplish this.

- Open the iTunes app and choose **File** > **Add Files to Library**.
- Connect the iPhone or iPad
- Click on the images from the folder on the hard drive where they are saved.
- Select **Photos and Videos** from the menu at the top of iTunes, check the boxes next to each item you want to upload, and then click the **Sync button**.

Setting The Organizer preferences

You only need to follow the steps below to configure the organizer settings.

- Go to the **Edit** menu, and select **Preference**
- In the dialog box, you can make the necessary changes to the Organizer Preference. When you are done, click on **Ok.**

CHAPTER SIX

ORGANIZING YOUR PICTURES WITH ORGANIZER

By carefully reading the overview of the Organizer workspace, how to organize files, how to add icons to tags, and how to work with custom tags, etc. in this chapter, we will learn more about the organizer.

Getting Acquainted With The Overview of The Organizer Workspace

In this chapter, we will learn more about the organizer by carefully reviewing the workplace overview, how to arrange files, and how to add icons to tasks Before we learn how to use the Organizer workspace to organize photos, let's have a look at it.

The following are the things that are shown when you open an organizer: using custom tags, etc.

- ✦ **Menu Bar**: The Menu bar contains the commands for carrying out activities or operations in the Organizer. File. File, Edit, Find, View, and Help Menu are the commands that can be found in the menu bar.

- ✦ **Search Bar:** Images and other media objects can be located using this. To find images or media, type a search term into the Search drop-down menu.

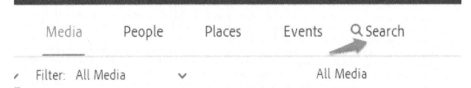

- ✦ **Sort By** This function allows you to sort your media by the most recent, oldest, names, and batches of photos loaded or imported into the Organizer.

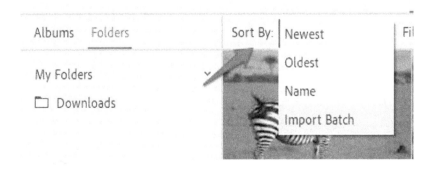

✦ **Features Buttons:** These are buttons that contain the Maximize, Minimize, and Close buttons. For Windows, these buttons are positioned at the top-right corner of the Organizer. For Mac, these buttons are positioned on the left-hand side.

✦ **Import:** You can import media files from files and folders, cameras, card readers, and scanners.

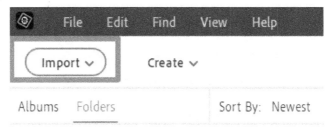

✦ **The Share:** This is located on the far right side of the Home screen. You may use this button to make and share calendars, collages, and more.

✦ **The Create Button:** This button is located beside the Open bar. This is used to create content such as Slide show, Photo Collage, Photo Reels, Quote graphics, etc.

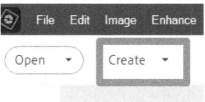

✦ **Album/Folder Tabs:** Every photo album created in your Organizer can be found in the Album/Folder Tabs.

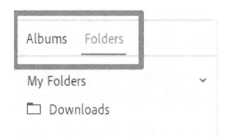

My Folders

    Downloads

* **Ratings/Auto Curator:** Giving your image or media asset a star rating is the job of the rating feature. Ratings are another tool you may use to arrange and classify media files and photos. You can use the Auto Curator to automatically analyze the image and look for visual patterns.

* **Folder View:** To access the images in each folder, select the Folder name to see them.

✦ **Media Browsers:** The thumbnails of the images imported into the organizer are displayed by the Media browser.

✦ **Keynote/Info:** It permits one to access the Panel bin and then select Options from the Tags or information

✦ **Hide Panel:** This option allows you to conceal the left panel in the Media Browser, which is useful when you want to see all of the photo thumbnails.

✦ **Undo/Rotate:** This option allows you to rotate an image clockwise and counterclockwise. Here also, you get to undo or redo an action by clicking on a tiny arrow.

✦ **Add Location:** In the Organizer, this is where you can create a new location. When you select this option, a window appears at the top of the Organizer, displaying the new location, which is then added to the Places panel.

✦ **Add Event:** This is another feature in the Organizer that allows you to organize images.

✦ **Instant Fix:** This tool aids in the application of Quick Edit adjustments to your photos. You can crop, fix red-eye, adjust lighting, and more using Instant Fix.

✦ **Editor:** This icon you can return to the Photo Editor

✦ **Slideshow:** To create a project called Memory, click on the Slideshow button. The images are displayed as videos in the Slideshow.

- **Home Screen**: When you click on this button, you are referred back to the Home screen.
- **Zoom**: The size of thumbnails is reduced or magnified using the Zoom feature.

The Views Tabs in the Organizer

There are four view tabs on the organizer in Photoshop Element. These perspective tabs let you organize and show your media according to the people who are in the pictures, the places where they were taken, and the things that happened while the pictures were being taken.

The Organizer's numerous perspectives tabs are listed below.

- **Media**: This is a location where all the media files are displayed or exhibited. Here in this view, you can also make changes to your images.
- **People**: This view tab allows you to view images based on who is in them (**people**). You can also organize the images of the people that appear in them.
- **Places**: This view tab allows you to view images based on the location or places where they are taken. You can also organize the images according to the location or place where they are taken
- **Events**: You can construct a stack of events in this view, each of which contains an image of the event. Creating an event for a birthday celebration, for example, and tagging the images from the occasion within it.

Using Tags to Sort Images into Groups

When photos are categorized, they are typically easier to manage in the organizer, and tags are a terrific way to keep your photos organized. The time that an image was captured can be used to analyze and classify it, among other things.

The Tags panel divides tags into four groups: **Keywords**, **People Tags, Places Tags**, and **Events Tags**.

Creating And Viewing Tag

Follow the steps below to create a new tag.

- ✦ Open Your **Media Browser** and select the images you desire to tag.
- ✦ Click on the drop-down arrow beside the **New** button (the New button is a plus sign) to create a new tag.
- ✦ Click on **New Category** in the drop-down menu

✦ Specify the category you want in the category listed by clicking on the **Category** drop-down menu.

✦ Enter the tag`s name in the **Name text box** and add a description in the **Note text box.**

✦ Then click on **Ok**

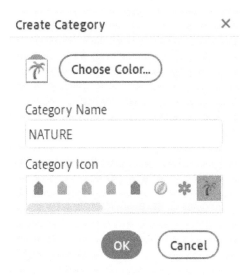

Adding Icons To Tags

Follow the steps below to successfully add an icon to a tag.

- ✦ Visit the **Tags section** and select the **New** button (it resembles a **green plus sign**).
- ✦ Select **New Keyword Tag** from the drop-down menu;
- ✦ Select **Edit Icon** from the **Create Keyword Tag dialog box**.
- ✦ In the **Edit Keyword Tag Icon** dialog box, click on **the Import button** to navigate through the folder to find the image to use as the icon
- ✦ To return to the **Edit Keyword Tag Icon**, select the desired image
- ✦ then click Open. Then click the **Ok** button.

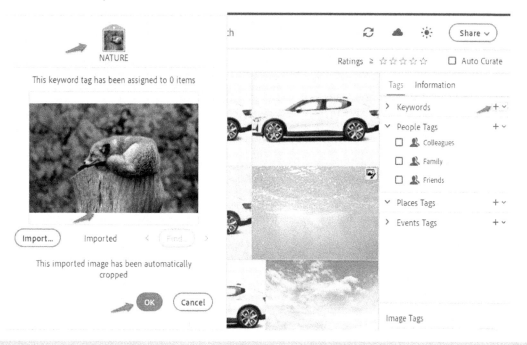

Customs Tags and Their Uses

Custom tags are those made in the Tags panel. We'll go through a few commands from the Tag panel's drop-down menu in this section that are useful when generating custom tags.

- ✦ **New Keyword Tag**: As earlier discussed, the New Keyword Tag is used to create a new tag.

- **New Sub Category**: This is a tag that appears within another tag. To make a subcategory, follow the steps below.
  - Select **New Sub-Category** from the **New menu**
  - **In the dialog box, enter the name of the new subcategory**
- **New Category:** This gives you the option of creating a new category. To make a new category, open the dialog box by clicking New Category, and then type in the name of the new category.
- **Edit**: This option allows you to access the Edit Keyword dialog box. Here in this Edit option, you can add icons to a tag
- **Import Keyword Tags From File:** This is useful when you've invested time and effort categorizing files, creating a new catalog, importing photographs, and also importing tags for the photos. Any tag that is exported or imported has an XML file attached to it.
- **Save Keyword Tags To A File:** You can store tags in a file and retrieve them later with this option. You can import the same collection names produced in one catalog file to another catalog file when you open a different catalog file.
- **Collapse All keyword Tags:** This feature allows you to collapse the list where the Tags are displayed.
- **Expand All Keyword Tags:** This expands the collapsed list that contains the tag.
- **Show Large Icon:** Clicking on this option changes the tags icon to be displayed into a larger icon in the Tags panel.

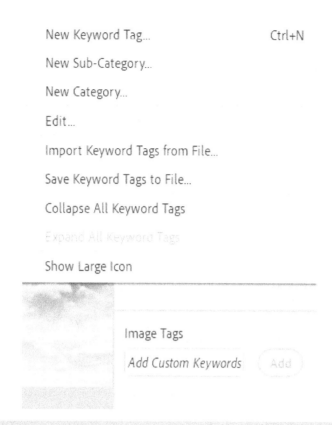

New Keyword Tag...   Ctrl+N

New Sub-Category...

New Category...

Edit...

Import Keyword Tags from File...

Save Keyword Tags to File...

Collapse All Keyword Tags

Expand All Keyword Tags

Show Large Icon

Image Tags

Add Custom Keywords   Add

Auto Curating Images

The Auto Curator looks for visual similarities between images. The top images are displayed in the Media Browser once the assessments are complete. The Auto Curator check box is located in the upper-right area of the Organizer pane.

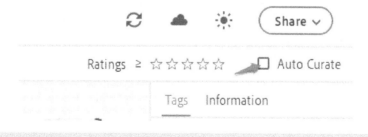

Ratings ≥ ☆☆☆☆☆   ☐ Auto Curate

Tags   Information

Auto-Creation at Work

It is advisable to familiarize yourself with Auto Creation, which is used to create various events in your images, to gain a thorough understanding of Auto Creation's capabilities.

♦ Go to **Organizer Preference** in the **Edit menu** and select **Media Analysis**

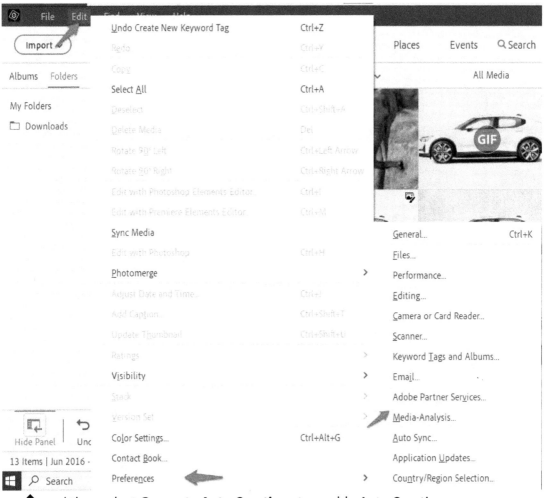

	File	Edit		

Undo Create New Keyword Tag	Ctrl+Z
Redo	Ctrl+Y
Copy	Ctrl+C
Select All	Ctrl+A
Deselect	Ctrl+Shift+A
Delete Media	Del
Rotate 90° Left	Ctrl+Left Arrow
Rotate 90° Right	Ctrl+Right Arrow
Edit with Photoshop Elements Editor	Ctrl+I
Edit with Premiere Elements Editor	Ctrl+M
Sync Media	
Edit with Photoshop	Ctrl+H
Photomerge	>
Adjust Date and Time...	Ctrl+J
Add Caption...	Ctrl+Shift+T
Update Thumbnail	Ctrl+Shift+U
Ratings	>
Visibility	>
Stack	>
Version Set	>
Color Settings...	Ctrl+Alt+G
Contact Book...	
Preferences	>

Import

Albums Folders

My Folders

📁 Downloads

Places   Events   🔍 Search

All Media

GIF

General...	Ctrl+K
Files...	
Performance...	
Editing...	
Camera or Card Reader...	
Scanner...	
Keyword Tags and Albums...	
Email...	
Adobe Partner Services...	
Media-Analysis...	
Auto Sync...	
Application Updates...	
Country/Region Selection...	

Hide Panel   Und

13 Items | Jun 2016 -

🔍 Search

⬍ and then select **Generate Auto Creations** to enable Auto Creation.

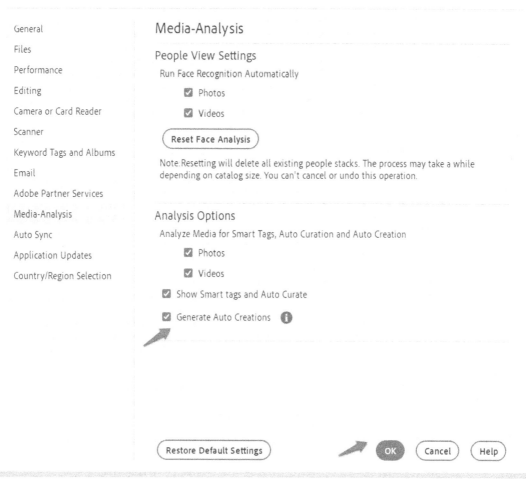

General

Files

Performance

Editing

Camera or Card Reader

Scanner

Keyword Tags and Albums

Email

Adobe Partner Services

Media-Analysis

Auto Sync

Application Updates

Country/Region Selection

Media-Analysis

People View Settings

Run Face Recognition Automatically

☑ Photos

☑ Videos

(Reset Face Analysis)

Note:Resetting will delete all existing people stacks. The process may take a while depending on catalog size. You can't cancel or undo this operation.

Analysis Options

Analyze Media for Smart Tags, Auto Curation and Auto Creation

☑ Photos

☑ Videos

☑ Show Smart tags and Auto Curate

☑ Generate Auto Creations 🛈

(Restore Default Settings)   OK (Cancel) (Help)

Adding New Events

In your Media Browser, you can add a brand-new event. All you have to do to do this is click **Add New Event** in the bottom left corner of the organizer. Click **OK** after entering the name, start date, end date, and description as they appear in the dialogue window.

Add New Event

Name: Academic Conference:

Start Date: 10/24/2023

End Date: 10/24/2023

Group: None

Description:

13 Items

Done   Cancel

Using Stars to Rate Images

The Organizer allows users to rank images by giving them one to five stars. One star is the lowest and five stars are the best rating. You can also sort out your images according to their ratings.

To rate a photo with a star

- ✦ From the **Media Browser**, select the photo
- ✦ Go to the Ratings option at the right-hand side of the screen to click one or two-star, depending on what you are rating.

Ratings ≥ ★ ☆ ☆ ☆ ☆   ☐ Auto Curate

Filter media based on star ratings

Name: Academic Conference:

Making Use of Photo Albums

The albums available in the Element Organizer are fairly comparable to the conventional albums where you may save and arrange your images. With albums, you may group your photos according to tags and star ratings, for example. More than one photo can be added to the album, and it can also be deleted.

Creating an Album

To create an album of your choice within the Organizer, follow the steps below

- ✦ Select the images you wish to add to the album
- ✦ Click on **Album** at the left-hand side of the Organizer
- ✦ Click on the **plus (+)** sign and then select **New Album**

- ✦ At the right-hand side of the panel, enter the name of the album in the **Name text box,** and also categorize the album in the **Category drop-down menu.**

New Album

Album Name:

Animal images |

Category:

None (Top Level)   ⌄

1 Item

OK   Cancel

• When you're finished, click the **OK** button, and the photographs will appear on the Media browser's left side.

Creating An Album Category

Follow the steps below to create an album category.

◆ Click on **Album** at the left-hand side of the Organizer
◆ Click on the **plus (+)** sign and then select **New Album Category**

* On the panel's right-hand side, in the **Name text box** and **Category drop-down menu**, respectively, enter the album's name and category.
* Next, click **OK**.

NOTE: *You can add photos to an album by doing any of the following*

* Drag the photos from the Media view into the album in the Album panel
* Drag the album from the Album panel to the photo in the Media view
* You can also select the stack and drag it to the album.

Browsing Through an Album of Photos

To view the photos in an album, double-click on the album

Deleting an Album

You can delete an album from the Album panel by following the steps provided below:

- Right-click on the album and select **Delete**

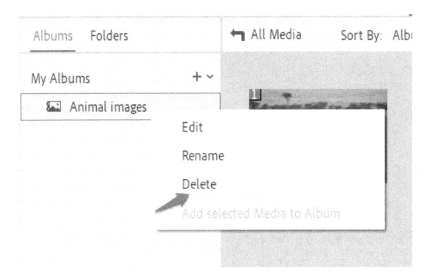

- In the **Confirm Album Deletion** dialog box, click on **Ok** to delete the Album

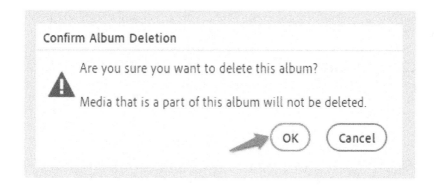

Removing an Image from an Album

You can remove an image from an album by following the steps provided below

- Right-click on the image to be removed from the Album
- Then choose **Remove From Album** and then click on **Remove**

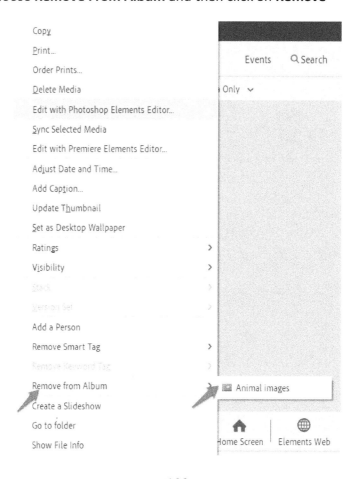

Sorting Photos in an Album

You can use reverse chronological, chronological, or album sorting methods to arrange the photos in your album. The procedures below can be used to sort the images in an album.

- ⬍ Select an album from the **Album** and **Folders panel**
- ⬍ In the **Sort By** drop-down menu in the Media view, select any of the following options

  - ○ **Newest:** With this choice, the photographs are arranged by date, going from most recent to oldest.
  - ○ **Oldest:** With this selection, the images are arranged chronologically from oldest to newest.
  - ○ **Name:** This option alphabetizes the media from A to Z by name.
  - ○ **Import Batch:** This option arranges the photos in batches based on when they were imported
  - ○ **Album Order:** This option arranges the images according to the user's preferences.

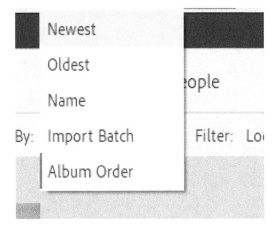

CHAPTER SEVEN

VIEWING AND FINDING YOUR IMAGES

The catalog and how to browse and arrange your images in the Organizer will be the main topics of discussion in this chapter. You'll discover how to view slideshows and do image searches in the Organizer. Now let's look at this chapter.

Cataloging A File

A catalog is a file in the Element that has a record of all the imported content; the organizer names the default catalog My Catalog. Basic information about the imported material, such as its location and filename, are automatically updated in the catalog when media is loaded.

The catalog file contains the following details:

- The name and location of any associated audio files
- The location of the original and full-resolution file as well as its filename, filename, and volume name.
- The location and name of the unaltered original file
- The title of the camera or scanner connected to the group of imported media files
- Inclusion of captions in the media file
- The alterations made to the media file's notes
- The media file, including images, videos, audio files, and projects
- When the media file was created, both the date and time
- Adding keyword tags to the media file
- The Album that houses the media file.
- A media file's history.
- • The modifications made to the media file. Cropping, removing red-eye, rotating, and other editing techniques are used.
- • The size in pixels of each image and video file.
- • The project's parameters.
- • Metadata, including pixel sizes, EXIF, copyright, IPTC data, and file format data.

Creating A Catalog

You must first become comfortable with the Catalog Manager before you can build a new catalog. Catalogs are created, removed, and managed in the catalog manager. All you have to do to make a catalog is adhere to the straightforward instructions given below:

- Go to the **File menu** and click on **Manage Catalogs**

- In the **Catalog Manager** dialog box, click **on New**

- Enter the name of the new catalog in the **File Name** text box and then click on **Ok**

Images can now be added to created catalogs. Follow the steps below to add images to the catalog you have created.

- Browse your hard drive and select the image you want to add in the **Get Photo and Videos** dialog box by choosing it from the right-hand side of the Get Photo and Videos menu under the **File** menu.
- Then click the **Get Media button**.

Launching a Catalog

Follow the instructions below to open/launch a catalog.

- Go to the **File menu** and click on **Manage Catalogs**
- In the **Catalog Manager** dialog box, click on **My Catalog**
- Afterwards, click **Open**

Making Use of the Catalog

After successfully generating a catalog, keep the following vitals in mind while you work with the catalog.

- ✦ You'll need to know how to classify your photographs once you've made a catalog. You must manually divide catalogs into smaller or larger categories by copying and pasting photographs from an older catalog into the new one because Element does not by default have a method for doing so.
- ✦ How to move from one discourse to the next is another crucial thing to keep in mind. Navigate to **File**, choose **Manage Catalogs**, click the name of the catalog you wish to open, and then click the **Open** button to switch between them.
- ✦ After you've made your first catalog, consider how to repair a damaged catalog. The catalog has been corrupted if you are unable to open your photos in editing mode or view the thumbnail preview of them. The damaged catalog will be fixed using the **Repairs button**. To do this, go to **File**, choose **Manage Catalogs**, and then click the names of the catalogs you want to open, fix, and open. Finally, click the Repair button next to the catalog you want to repair.
- ✦ Improving the performance of your catalog can help it run more quickly and smoothly. You must continually optimize your catalog if you want to increase its performance. Navigate to File, choose Manage Catalogs, and then select the Optimize option.

Creating a Backup of Your Catalog

The backup of a catalog is far more important than building and updating one. By backing up your catalog, you may remove the concern of data loss resulting from corruption or error on your devices. Although you can backup your library on a Mac or Windows computer, you can only use a CD or DVD to back up the Elements catalog on a Windows computer.

To back up your catalog, follow the procedure below,

- ✦ Go to **File** and click on **Backup Catalog**
- ✦ **In the Backup Catalog dialog box**, choose any of the options below and click on the **Next** button.
  - o **Backup Catalog Structure:** This option allows you to back up the structure of your catalog including the tags, people, places, and events. Here, the photos and videos are not included in the backup.

- ○ **Full Backup:** When you're going to do your first backup or write files to a new media source, this option is chosen. In a nutshell, this option backs up everything in your catalog including the photos and images.
- ○ **Incremental Backup:** When you've completed at least one backup and want to update the files you've backed up, this option is selected.

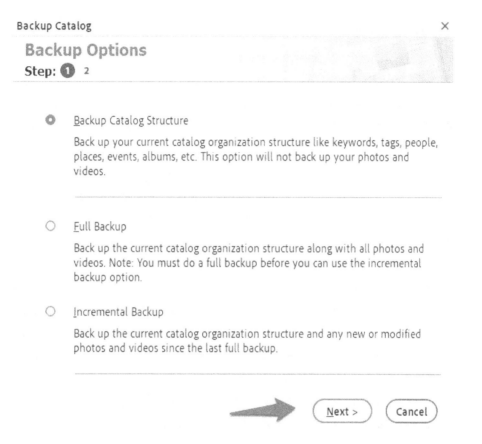

- In the next screen, select the **Destination Drive** by clicking the desired drive letter
- Under **Options**, click on **Browse** to the location to save the backup catalog, and then click on **Ok**
- Finally, click on the **Save Backup** button to finish the backup

Backup Catalog   ✕

Destination Settings

Step: 1 ❷

Select Destination Drive

C:

Options

Backup Path: C:\   (Browse...)

Previous Backup file: (Browse...)

Size: 1.70 MB

(< Back) (Save Backup) (Cancel)

Restoring A Catalog

It is important to know that only catalogs that have been backed up can be retrieved or restored. Follow the procedures below to restore a catalog.

- Navigate to **File** and click on **Restore Catalog**
- You can either click on **CD/DVD** or **Hard Drive** or **Other Volume** from the **Restore Catalog** dialog box. Click on browse to find where your backup file is located if it is Hard Drive you chose.
- After selecting the backup file, click on **Browse** on the **Restore Files and Catalog** to set the location to restore the backed-up file
- You can click on Restore Original Folder Structure to maintain the files that are contained in the catalog
- Then click on the **Restore button.**

Restore Catalog from CD, DVD, or Hard Drive   ✕

Restore From

○ CD/DVD

Select Drive   ⌄

◉ Hard drive / Other Volume

Locate the Backup File: <NONE>   (Browse...)

Restore to

Specify Destination: <NONE>   (Browse...)

☑ Restore Original Folder Structure

☑ Do not sync media to the Adobe cloud.   (Restore)   (Cancel)

Creating A Backup of your Photos and Files

To back up your photos and files, follow the procedures below:

- Navigate to the File menu and click on **Copy/Move to removable**.

- In the dialog box that opens, click on **Copy Files** and select **Next.**

- Select a hard drive, input the name of the backup folder, and then click on **OK.**

Changing from one view to another

The Organizer offers you diverse different viewing options right in the View tab.

To access different viewing options, go to the View tab and select any of the following.

- **Media Types**: This option allows you to remove the video, music, and PDF files from the Media Brower and replace them with photographs, and vice versa. Go to **View**, select **Media Brower**, and then select the submenu
- **Hidden Files:** Here you can hide your files in the View tab. To view all files, go **to View,** and select **All Files.**
- **Details:** By default, file information such as file creation dates and star ratings are concealed. The o view details of a file, go to **View** and select **Details.**

- **File Name:** You can view the filename of your photos in the Media browser by choosing **View** and selecting **Files Names.** By default, the filenames of a photo are not displayed.
- **Timeline:** This is displayed in the horizontal bar at the top of the Organizer, where you can move the slider to the left or right to select when the time the picture was taken. To use this option, go to View and click on **Timeline**

Using a Slide Show (Memories) to view PAt

Tally still-image-based video is referred to as a slide show. The slide show enables the images to change from one shape to another in a variety of ways while keeping the shots in a logical order. The slide show is a striking method of displaying your photos. You might incorporate activities or sounds to make it more enjoyable.

There are three places you may find the slide show.

- At the bottom left-hand side of the **Media Browser** the **Editor**

117

- In the **Create Panel** within the **Media Browser**
- When you go to view selected photos in the **View tab**

Follow the procedure below to display images in a slideshow

- Select the pictures you wish to add to the slide show, select the **Create** button, and then click on **Slideshow** from the **Create** drop-down menu.

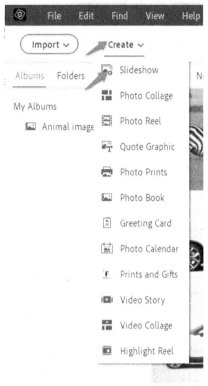

Open the slideshow preview using the images already in the slideshow window.

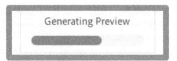

- When the slide show is displayed, you can add audio, themes, and media to your slide ow by clicking on **Audio**, **Themes**, **Media** within the Toolbar at the left side of the slideshow.

- To save the slide show, click on **Save**
- In the **Element Organizer dialog box,** enter the name of the slide show and then click on the **Save button**

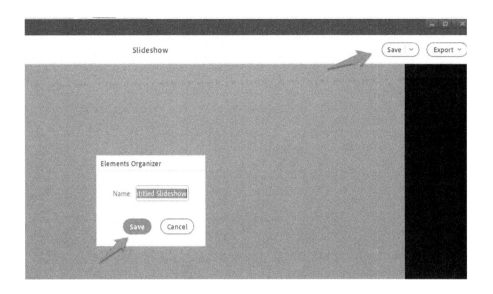

Searching For Photos

When looking for your photographs in the same place where you saved them, you might need to search the Element.

In this tutorial, we'll explore the various ways to search for images in Adobe Photoshop Element.

Using The Search Icon

The first thing to consider when looking through photos is the Search Icon. In the upper right corner is the Media Browser's search bar. There is a text area and a magnifying glass on the Search icon. Type the name of the image into the Search icon to locate it.

When you click on the Search icon, a window is displayed on the left-hand side, showing a list of parameters you can use to execute your search.

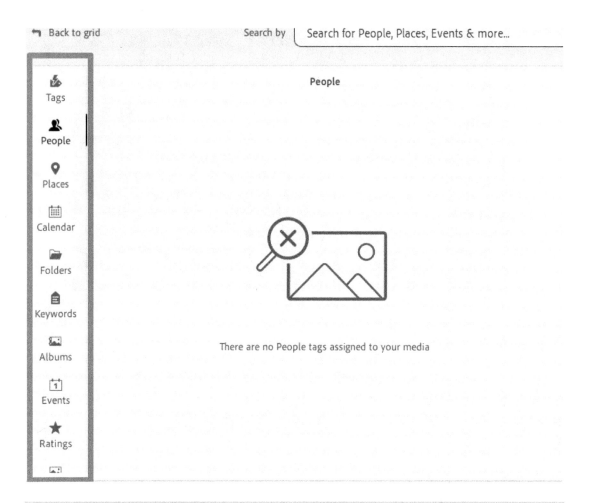

Displaying Recent Searches

The **Recent Searches** section displays a list of your most recent searches. Click on the search text bar to see the previous searches you have made.

Searching for Untagged Items

Another technique to locate your photographs in Element is to use the Untagged Command. Go to the Find menu and choose Untagged Items to utilize the Untagged Items command to find photographs.

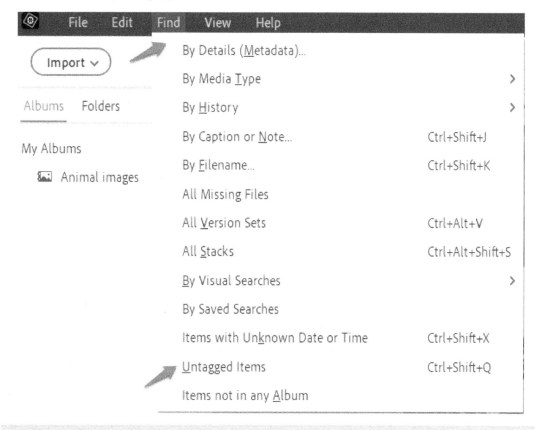

Searching For Caption and Notes

Using captions and annotations, you may look up photos. Additional information is provided in the Information panel via the captions and notes. When a caption or note is added, you can search for the image using the caption's or note's title.

Follow these steps to search photographs using captions and notes.

✦ Navigate to the **File menu** and click on **Captions and Notes**

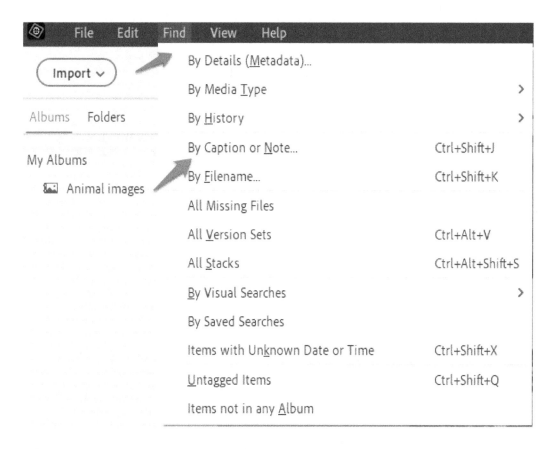

- **In the Find by Caption or Dialog box,** enter the word you wish to search. There are two options in this dialog box which are
  - **Match Only the Beginning of Words in Captions and Notes:** This is used when you are certain the caption or note starts with the words typed in the text box
  - **Match Any Part of Any Word in Captions and Notes**: This is used when you are not sure if the word entered into the text box is used at the start of the caption or note
- Then click on **Ok**

123

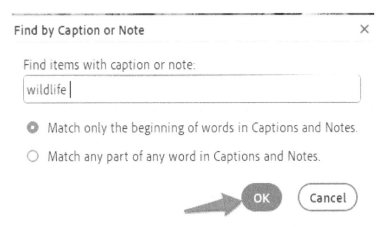

Searching By History

Using the Media Browser's activities as a starting point, you can search for photos here. Examples include printing, emailing, and sharing. Select any of the choices in the **History** submenu after selecting **Find**, **History**, and then History.

Searching By Metadata

When you wish to search for photographs based on several different criteria, using the metadata search is useful. People, places, events, filename, file type, tags, albums, notes, authors, capture date, camera model, shutter speed, and F-shop are the criteria used by the metadata.

Follow the steps below to use the metadata search.

✦ Go to **Find** and select **By Details (Metadata)**

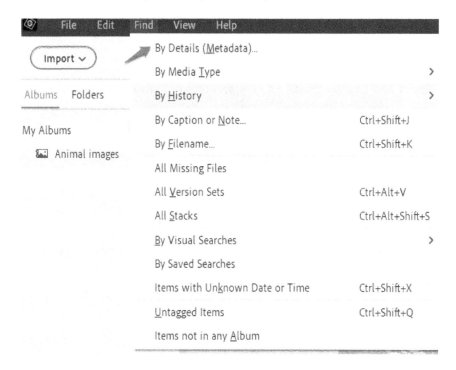

✦ **In the Search Criteria**, under **the Search For Files which Match,** select either **AND or OR**

✦ Select the metadata type in the first menu

✦ select the range for the search in the second menu

✦ In the third menu, you can type or select the metadata name that you wish to find

✦ To add metadata values to your search, click on the plus sign (+) at the right hand of the third menu.

✦ To remove the metadata from the search, click on the minus (-) sign at the right of the third menu

- You can activate **Save This Search As Saved** and then input the search.
- Then click on **Search**

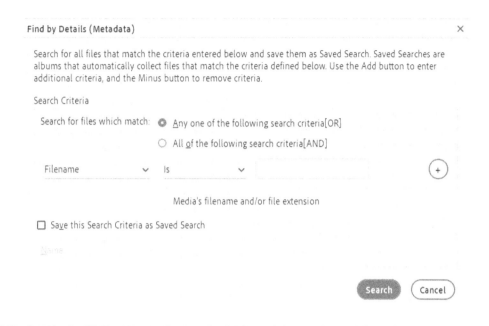

Find by Details (Metadata)   ✕

Search for all files that match the criteria entered below and save them as Saved Search. Saved Searches are
albums that automatically collect files that match the criteria defined below. Use the Add button to enter
additional criteria, and the Minus button to remove criteria.

Search Criteria

Search for files which match: ● Any one of the following search criteria[OR]

                                ○ All of the following search criteria[AND]

Filename   ⌄   Is   ⌄   (+)

                       Media's filename and/or file extension

☐ Save this Search Criteria as Saved Search

Name

                                                            Search   Cancel

Searching Media Type

You can use the media type to search for your photos as well. Go to Find, select By **Media Type**, and then select one of the methods below to find your photographs using the media file.

- **Photos**: This only displays pictures
- **Video:** This only display displays the thumbnails of video clips
- **Audio**: This displays an audio clip
- **Project**: This displays projects
- **Item With Audio Captions:** This displays the photo and projects to which the audio captions are attached.

Searching By Filename

Images can also be found via filename searches. Use the steps below to search for photos.

- Go to **File** and select **Filename**
- Enter the name of the file in the Filename dialog box and then click on **Ok**

Searching By All Missing Files

You can use this to look for missing files in your creations or projects. Go to **Find** and choose **All Files** to access the Missing Files option.

Searching By All Version Set

Searching for images using the All Version Set allows the Organizer to show the top photos of each set. With this, you can expand each set as you desire. To use the All Version Set, follow the instructions below

- ✦ Go to **Find**, and select **All Version Sets**
- ✦ You can expand a version set to right-click or control-click by selecting **Version Set,** and clicking on **Expand Items In Version Set**

Searching By All Stacks

To use the All Stacks option, go to the **Find** menu and click on **All Stacks.**

Searching by Using Visual Searches

When searching for images based on visual searches, the organizer makes use of information in the photo such as color, shape, and objects during the search. To use the visual searches, follow the procedures below

- Go to **Find**, and select **By Visual Searches**
- Then click on the **By Virtual Searches Submenu**

Searching Item with Unknown Date or Time

This allows the Organizer to display the media files in which the date or time set is unknown

To use this option, follow the steps below

- Go to **Find** and click on **Items With Unknown Date Or Time**

Searching for Unanalyzed Content

To search using this option, follow the steps below

- Go to **Find** and click on **Unanalyzed Content (All** the media files that are yet to be analyzed will be displayed)

Searching for Items, not in any Albums

There are times you will need to locate images that are not saved in an album. To locate such images, go to **Find** and click on **Items Not in Any Album**

Hiding Files

You might decide to conceal certain files, including photos while working on files directly from the Organizer. You only need to follow the below-listed instructions to do this;

- Select the files you wish to hide
- Go to the **Edit** menu, click on **Visibility,** and select **Mark as Hidden.**
- To unhide the files, follow the steps above and click on **Show Hidden.**

Stacking Up images

You can arrange your desired photographs in a single location in the Organizer by stacking them. When stacking images, only the first image that is chosen is seen, with the remaining images being buried behind it.

To stack your images, follow the steps provided below:

- Go to **the Organizer** and select the images you wish to stack
- Go to the **Edit** menu, click on **Stack,** and select **Stack Selected Photos**.

By Details (Metadata)...

By Media Type   >

By History   >

By Caption or Note...   Ctrl+Shift+J

By Filename...   Ctrl+Shift+K

All Missing Files

All Version Sets   Ctrl+Alt+V

All Stacks   Ctrl+Alt+Shift+S

By Visual Searches   >

By Saved Searches

Items with Unknown Date or Time   Ctrl+Shift+X

Untagged Items   Ctrl+Shift+Q

Items not in any Album

CHAPTER EIGHT

EDITING CAMERA IMAGES USING THE CAMERA EDITOR

The Camera Raw Editor

The Camera Raw Editor plug-in, which is included with Adobe Element, allows for efficient and high-quality image editing. This application allows you to import and enhance raw photographs. Originally released in 2003, this program supports not only Adobe Photoshop Elements but also Adobe Photoshop and Adobe Lightroom.

The Camera Raw Editor transforms the raw data from the camera into an image. Camera Raw also allows you to edit photographs using a variety of comparable operations, such as cropping, sharpening, altering white balance, contrasting, and adding color and tone range.

The modifications made to the photographs are also non-destructive, which means that they may be undone and that the original files are kept in the condition they were in before the modifications were made. Every time a raw file is opened, the Camera Raw Editor is shown in a separate window.

Follow these steps to launch the Camera Raw Editor in Adobe Photoshop Element.

- Navigate to **File** and select **Open With Camera Raw Editor**

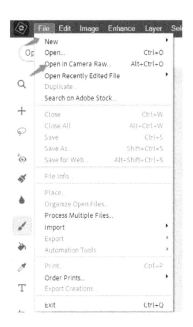

✦ Here on this page, the **Camera Raw Edito**r is displayed

Learning The Raw File Format Attributes

Images created by the digital camera are stored as raw files. The raw files, also known as digital negatives, are composed of unedited data collected directly from the camera's image sensor. Because they have more data than JPEG, these Raw files are larger. Raw files simply take up more space on your hard disk or memory cards because they are larger than JPEG files. Highlights, brightness, shadows, and dark portions of an image can all be adjusted separately in the raw data, which is something that cannot be done with the camera.

The ability to recover image information from the Raw file which is not possible from the JPEG file is another intriguing feature.

The Camera Raw files can be saved in the following formats:

✦ Nikon (. NEF)
✦ Canon (. CRW)
✦ Sony (. ARW . SRF)
✦ Pentax (. PEF)

- Olympus (. ORF)
- Hasselblad(.3FR)
- Panasonic(.RW2)

Getting Familiar With The Camera Raw Editor Window

The most significant aspects of the Camera Raw Editor in the Adobe Element will be covered in detail in this session, which will cover every aspect of the program.

The Title Bar: This shows the version of Camera Raw being installed in your Element; The Element 2024 uses version 15.5

Convert And Save Image Button: This opens you up to the Save Options dialog box where a copy of the camera raw image can be saved as DNG. This is located at the upper right-hand of the Camera Raw Editor windows.

Toggle Screen Full Mode Button: This button interchanges from the full screen to a smaller version in the Camera Raw dialog box.

Open Preferences Dialog button: This opens the Camera Raw Preferences dialog box

The Toolbar: This is located at the far right side of the Camera Raw dialog box. It contains the various tools used for editing in the Camera Raw Editor. From the top, we have Edit, Crop & Rotate, Eye removal, and More image settings. From the button, we have the Zoom and Hand tool toolbar of the Camera Raw dialog box.

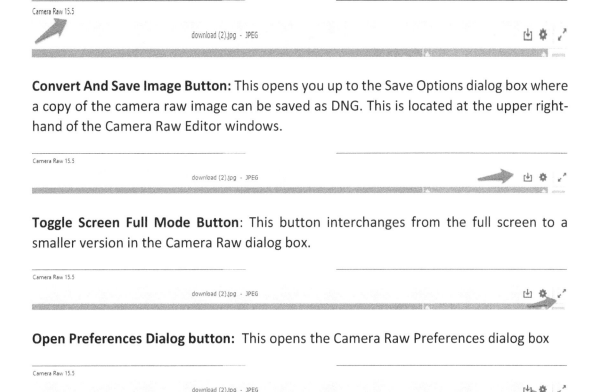

132

Histogram: This is located at the right corner of the Camera Raw dialog box. This feature allows you to keep watch on the overall tonal range of the raw file being worked on. Whatever changes are made from the Edit panel, it is being updated automatically on the histogram. On the upper left and right corners are the Shadow clipping warning and Highlight clipping warning. Found within the Histogram is the RGB

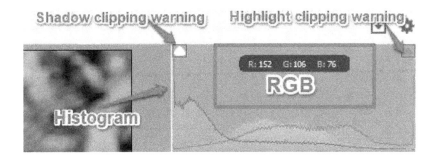

Shadow clipping warning   Highlight clipping warning

R: 152   G: 106   B: 76

RGB

Histogram

The Panels

The Panels are located below the Histogram at the right-hand side of the Camera Rae dialog. The Camera Raw Editor uses the panels to execute so many operations, just like the panels in Elements. The panels in the Camera Raw are located in one spot, making them easier to use. Now let's check out the panels in the Camera Raw Editor.

- ♦ **The Edit Panel:** This is used for making adjustments in the tab which automatically updates in the Histogram current image. This option makes use of the edit settings.

- ♦ **The Basic Panel:** This is the first panel to be displayed and it contains most of the features needed for editing the Raw files. At the top of this panel are control settings such as color temperature and white balance, with a group of sliders used for correcting the overall exposure, contrast, highlights, and shadows, and configuring the main white and black points. Right at the bottom of the Basic panel, is the Clarity slider to increase or decrease the contrast in mid-tones. Finally, there are the Vibrance and Saturation slides used for controlling color saturation.

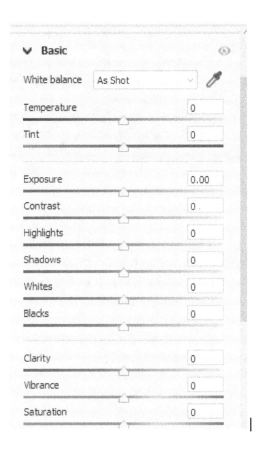

- **The Detail panel:** This is the third panel in the Camera Raw Editor. The top half of this panel is where you get to do your image sharpening, while the bottom half is where you get to reduce any luminance or color noise.

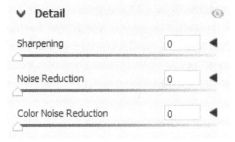

- **The Camera Calibration Panel:** Unlike the previous versions, The Camera Calibration is labeled The Calibration panel in Adobe Photoshop Elements 2024 and has improved and advanced features. The Calibration panel has five process versions in its panel. The current version of Photoshop Elements 2024 is version 6.

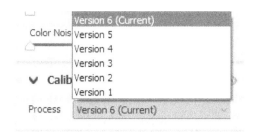

o **The Process Versions in The Calibration Panel:** The technique that Camera Raw employs to edit and output images is called **Process Version**. You have access to different options and settings in the Basic tab and when making local tweaks depending on the process version you are using. There are currently five process versions in the calibration panel.

- **Process Version 6:** This is the current version that was first in Camera Raw 15.4 and now it is being used in Camera Raw 15.5 of Photoshop Element 2024. This is used to reduce banding when the Color Mixer and B&W are being used.
- **Process Version 5:** Use Process Version 5 while editing fresh pictures in Camera Raw 11. Improved high ISO rendering in PV 5 helps to reduce purple color casts that can occasionally be seen in the shadows of photographs with less light. A better Dehaze slider is included in PV5. With this, adding haze for imaginative purposes is simple when the Dehaze slider is moved to the left.
- **Process Version 4:** Using process version 4, images are altered for the first time in Camera Raw 10. Range Mask support and a stronger Auto Mask that better manages image noise are added in PV 4. Images from PV 3 (2012) that do not have any Auto Mask changes made to them will be updated to PV 4 automatically.
- **Process Version 3(2012):** This panel is used to proffer solutions in the way the camera captures color. Here, there are Hue and Saturation sliders for all three primary colors (red, green, and blue). Here also is the Tint slider used for correcting shadows. At the top of this panel is the Process, which allows you to switch from Camera Raw's most recent image processing engine to other engines.
- **Process Version 2(2010):** Camera Raw 6 by default used PV 2 while editing images. Compared to the previous process version, PV 1, and PV 2 delivers better sharpness and noise reduction.
- **Process Version 1(2003): PV1** is version 5. x and previous versions of Camera Raw's original processing engine.

136

To update a photo from the previous Process Versions to the current Process version 5(PV 5), do either of the following:

- Click the **Update To Current Process** button (the exclamation-point icon) in the lower-right corner of the image preview.

- In the **Camera Calibration** tab, choose **Process** > **Version 6**(Current).

  To apply an older process version to a photo, go to the **Camera Calibration** tab and choose **Process**

  Version 4 >Process> Version 3 (2012), Process > Version 2 (2010), or **Process** > **Version 1 (2003)**.

Adjust Sharpness In-Camera Raw Files

The edge definition you want is provided by the sharpness slider, which adjusts the image's sharpness. Based on the threshold you provide, this adjustment finds pixels that are different from surrounding pixels and raises the contrast of those pixels by the specified amount.

To apply the sharpening to Raw file images, do the following

- Zoom the preview image to at least 100%
- Click on the Detail tab
- Move the Sharpness slider to the right to increase the sharpening and left to decrease the sharpening, when you move the slider to zero, the sharpening is turned off. Therefore, to have a cleaner image, let the Sharpness slider be set to a lower value.

Reducing Noise In-Camera Raw Image

The Camera Raw dialog box's Detail tab has a slider for lowering image noise. An unimportant visible object called picture noise degrades the quality of the image. The two types of image noise are chroma noise (color), which appears as colorful objects in the image, and luminance noise (grayscale), which gives the image a grainy appearance.

To reduce the image noise.

- Zoom the preview image to at least 100%
- Move the Luminance Smoothing slider to the right to reduce grayscale noise, and move the Color Noise Reduction slider to the right to reduce the chroma noise

The Adobe Camera Raw Profile

The profile determines how tones and colors are shown in Camera Raw images. The profile offers a starting point for image changes.

Click the **Edit button** in the **Toolbar** to the right of the Camera Raw dialog box in Photoshop Elements to view the current Camera Raw profile. You can also verify the Camera Raw profile in use by selecting it from the **Profile drop-down menu** in the **Edit panel**.

NOTE: The profile selected does not change the editing value set by the sliders that appear in the Basic and Detail panels. Therefore, you can apply a profile either before or after making any adjustments, without losing any adjustment values.

Applying Profile To Your Image

Follow the procedures below to apply a profile to your image,

◆ Go to the **Edit Panel Camera Raw** dialog box, and click on the **Profile drop-down menu to view the profiles. To see other available profiles**, click on **Browse.**

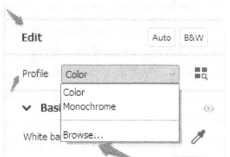

◆ Expand the profile group to view the profiles available in each group

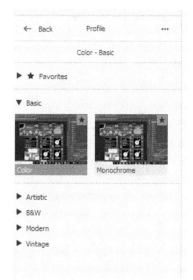

✦ Move the pointer over any profile to preview its effect in the image, and click the desired profile to apply it to your image.

Adding Profiles To Favorite

To add a profile to Favorite, select the profile thumbnail and then click on the star icon that appears at the upper corner of the thumbnail.

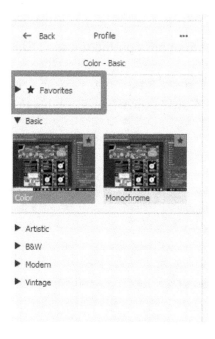

Creative Profiles For Raw and Non-Raw Photos

A creative profile is a profile made to give your image a certain look or feel. These profiles can be used with any file, and some of them support TIFF, JPEGS, and raw images.

- **Artistic:** This is used when you want the color rendering in your photo to be tenser and also with strong color shifts.
- **B & W:** When you need to get an optimal tone shift for a black-and-white project, this profile is best suited for it.
- **Modern**: This profile provides an outstanding effect that best suits modern photography styles.
- **Vintage:** This profile gives the effects of a vintage photo outlook

Profiles For Raw Photos

The following profile groups display when you are editing a raw profile

- Adobe Raw: This profile is designed to enhance the colors in your images as well as create a good foundation for editing. This is the default profile given to the raw images imported to the Camera Raw Editor.
- Camera Matching: This profile is displayed based on the camera make or model of your raw image. The Camera Matching profile is best used when you intend to make your raw images correlate with what is seen on the camera's display screen.
- Legacy: This profile is displayed in the earlier version of Adobe Camera Raw.

CHAPTER NINE

MAKING AND MODIFYING SELECTIONS

Making the most of Photoshop Element's Selections is one of the fundamental skills you can't afford to ignore.

This chapter will cover the concept of selection as well as the many tools and techniques available in Photoshop Element. We will also be taught the guidelines to adhere to when using the instruments for selection in any capacity.

Defining Selections

A selection is the area of the picture you wish to modify. Once a selection is made, the selected region can be edited. To create a selection, you can use the selection commands or the selection tools. Each time you make a selection, the selection border—a dotted outline—appears. You can modify, copy, or erase certain pixels from the image using the selection boundary. Remember that nothing can be done outside of the selected area until it is deselected.

You may make several selections using the selection tools in Adobe Photoshop Element. Examples of selection tools are the Magic Wand and Elliptical Marquee tools.

Creating Rectangular And Elliptical Selections

To create square or rectangular selection borders, developers built the Rectangular Marquee tool. Follow these procedures to choose this option using this tool.

- Go to the **Tools panel** and select the **Rectangular Marquee tool**
- The other options of the marquee tools appear at **The Tool options** at the footer panel

- Bring the mouse cursor to the area of the image where the corner of an imagery rectangle should be
- Drag the mouse from the area of the image you want to the opposite corner and then release the mouse for rectangular selection to display on the image.

The Elliptical Marquee Tool

To create elliptical or circular borders or selections, use the ellipse tool. The greatest objects to select with this tool are those that are spherical, like clocks, balloons, and other similar items.

142

Do the following to use the Elliptical marquee tool,

✦ After clicking on the **Marquee tool**, move to the **Tool Options** in the footer panel to click on the **Elliptical Marquee Tool.**

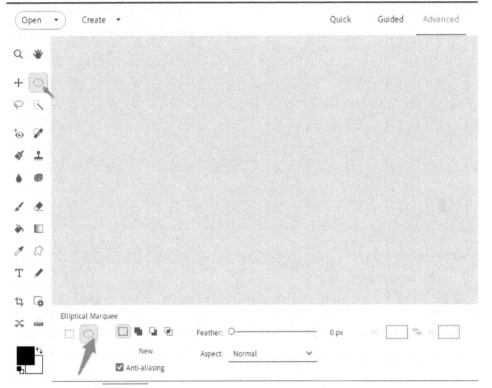

✦ Place the mouse to the area to the area to be selected, and then drag it around to the object you desire.

✦ Then, release the mouse button.

Using The Marquee Options

There are various features in the Marquee tools that will come in handy while using them. Let's now quickly review them.

- ✦ **Feather:** The focus of this option is to give the portion of the image that has been selected soft edges. The slider-adjustable value of the pixels, which ranges from 0 to 250, determines the degree of softness. The edges become softer the higher the value.
- ✦ **Anti-Aliasing:** By omitting the application of softening to the edge of the elliptical or irregular-shaped selection, this option aims to prevent the photos' rough edges from seeming harsh.
- ✦ **Aspect:** This option contains the following settings:
  - o Normal: This is the default setting, and it enables you to drag a selection to change its size to any value.
  - o Fixed Ratio: Using this option, you may choose a fixed width-to-height ratio.
  - o Fixed Size: You can set the width and height to any values you choose with this setting. When you need to choose several items that are all the same size, this choice is helpful.
- ✦ **Width(W) And Height(H):** The width and height text boxes' values are entered here. Click on the double-headed arrow between the width and height values to change the values.
- ✦ **Refine Edge:** This feature allows you to fine-tune the edges of your selection.

Making Selections With The lasso Tools

The Photoshop Element's lasso tools let you make any freehand selection, such as curves or sections with straight edges for polygon selection forms. The following categories:

- ✦ Lasso
- ✦ Polygonal
- ✦ Magnetic

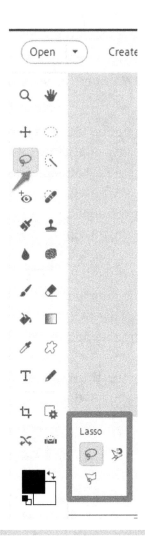

The Lasso Tool

The Lasso tool is used to make freehand selection borders on an image or object(s). Follow the procedure below to make a freehand selection.

- Go to the **Tools panel** and select the **Lasso tool**
- Move the mouse cursor to the object you wish to select and then outline it
- Then release the button to complete the selection

The Polygonal Lasso Tool

The Polygon Lasso tool is used to draw a straight-edged segment of a selection border. This tool allows you to create as many segments as you want to create a selection border. To use this tool, follow the procedures below

- Go to the **Tools panel** and select the **Polygon Lasso tool**
- Click on any point you want the first straight segment to start and then click again for the second time, where the segment will end. Then you can now start another one
- Then close the selection border.

The Magnetic Lasso Tool

When you drag your mouse over an object in a photo, the Magnetic Lasso Tool is utilized to form a selection border that extends to the boundaries of the object. This is useful if you want to select any object with intricate edges set against a background with lots of contrast.

To use the Magnetic lasso Tool, follow the procedures below,

- Go to the **Tools Panel** and select the Magnetic Lasso tool
- Move the mouse cursor to the **tools option** and select The **Magnetic lasso Tool.**
- Then move your mouse cursor around the object clicking
- Finally, move the mouse back to the starting point, and then close the selection

Working With The Magic Wand

The primary feature of The Magic Wand tool is used to select pixels inside an identical color range or boundary with a single click. With this tool, You can decide the color range or tolerance. The Tolerance value ranges from 0-255. The Area selected at tolerance range 0 will only have one color, but at Tolerance range 255, all the colors in the image will be selected.

Follow the steps below, to use The Magic Wand,

- ✦ Go to the **Tools panel** and select the **Quick Selection** tool
- ✦ Then, Select the **Magic Wand** tool in **the Tool options** in the **footer panel**

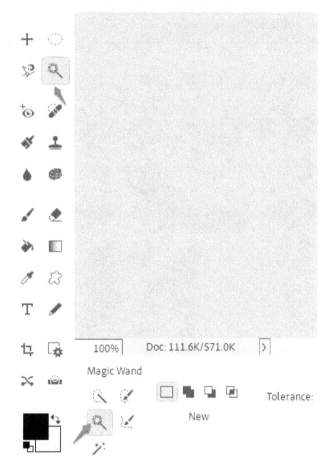

- ✦ Select anywhere on your image, making use of the default Tolerance setting.
- ✦ Set a new Tolerance setting in the Tool Options

You can maximize the features below in the Magic Wand before closing up

- o **Tolerance**: Its value ranges from 0 to 225, at range 0, the area will select only one color, but at range 255, all colors in the image will be selected.
- o **Sample All Layers**: This feature is best used when you have multiple layers. The Magic Wand tool will only select the pixels from the active layer if you don`t click on this option.

- o **Contiguous**: This feature allows the Magic Wand to choose pixels that are together with each other. When it is not enabled, not mining if they are adjacent to each other or not.
- o **Anti-aliasing:** This feature allows you to unstiffen the edge of the selection by one column of pixels.
- o **Refine Edge:** It allows to remove roughness from the edges using the Smooth slider.
- ◆ Then click on the image again to close.

Painting With The Selection Brush

The Selection Brush tool allows you to use another selection tool before it begins to fine-tune the selection by either adding or removing pixels in or out of the selection. These tools give you two ways for making selections; it is either you paint over the area you wish to choose in the Selection mode, or you paint on the area you do not wish to choose to make use of a semi-opaque overlay in Mask mode.

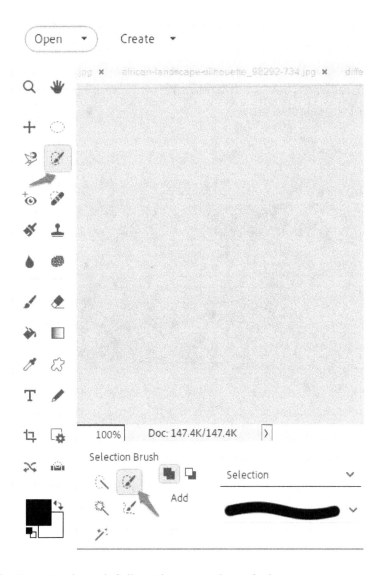

To use the Selection Brush tool, follow the procedures below.

- ☘ Go to the **Tools Panel** and select the **Selection Brush** tool.
- ☘ Set the **Selection Brush** options in the **Tool Option.**
    - o **Mode:** This permits you to choose Selection if you want to paint over what you desire to select, or Mask if you don`t want to paint over the part you don`t want.
    - o **Brush Presets Picker:** You select a brush from the presets drop-down list from this option.

- o **Size:** It permits you to set the size of the brush ranging from 1 to 2,500 pixels. You can either enter the value or drag the slider.
- o **Hardness:** This feature permits you to determine the hardness of the brush tip, ranging from 1 to 100 percent.
- ◆ Then paint the selected area.

Painting With The Quick Selection Key

When you click on the region you desire to pick, the Quick Selection tools enable you to make a selection based on the texture and color similarities. One may compare the Quick Selection tool to a hybrid of the Brush, Magic Wand, and Lasso tools.

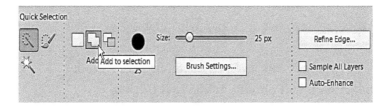

Follow the steps below to use the Quick Selection:

- ◆ Go to the **Tools panel** and select the **Quick Selection Brush** tool
- ◆ Set the options in the **Tool Options**
  New Selection: This is the default option that allows you to create a new selection

Size: You get to choose your desired brush size by setting the diameter from 1 to 2,500 pixels

Brush Settings: These settings allow you to set the hardness, spacing, angle, and roundness of the usage of the Quick Selection Brush tool.

Sample All Layers: This option allows you to make a selection from all layers in the image. If this option is not selected, you can only make a selection from the active layer.

Auto Enhance: This option helps Element to improve the selection automatically, by introducing an algorithm

- Paint the area of the image you want

- You can also add or delete from your selections

- To fine-tune your selection, click on the Refine Edge in the Tool Options, and then change the settings as you like

Working With Auto Selection Tool

When you create a shape around the image you chose, the Auto Selection Tool is also used to create a selection. Rectangle, Ellipse, Lasso, and Polygon Lasso are some of the tools included in the Auto Selection tool.

Follow the procedures below, to use the Auto Selection tool.

- Go to the **Tools panel** and select the **Auto Selection Brush** tool

- In the Tools Options bar, select any of the following options

  o New Selection: This allows you to draw a new selection and it is the default setting.

  o Add to selection: This allows you to add to the existing selection

  o Subtract from the selection: This allows you to remove from an already existing selection

- Click on any of the following tools to draw around the object you desire (Rectangle, Ellipse, Lasso, and Polygon Lasso)

- Draw around the object you wish to select in the photo

- You can add, remove or start a new selection to refine the selection.

- You can also click on Refine Edge to make further corrections on your selections as well as make them precise.

Using The Refine Selection Brush Tool

By automatically detecting edges in the image, the Refine Selection Brush Tool allows you to add or remove any portion of your selection.

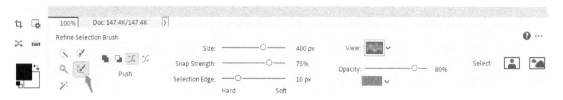

To use the Refine Selection Brush Tool, follow the steps below

- Click on the **Quick Selection tool** then afterward,
- Choose the **Refine Selection Brush** tool from the **Tools Option's** list of tools, which also includes the Quick Selection tool, Magic Wand, and Selection Brush.
- Set the following parameters in the Tool Options.

  o **Size:** This option allows the slider to correct the brush diameter ranging from 1 to 2,500 pixels

  o Snap Strength: This enables the slider to adjust the snap strength from 0 to 100%.

  o Selection Edge: This allows the slider to set how hard or soft the edge should be.

  o Add/Subtract: With this option, you can either add or subtract from the selection.

  o Push: With this option, you can move the mouse cursor within the selection to increase the selection right within the boundary of the outer circle of your cursor.

153

o Smooth: With this option, you can smoothen the edges of the selection when it becomes rough.

o View: With this option, you can view the selection. You can either view the selected object on a black or white background or you can use the Overlay to view it against a red semi-opaque

✦ After that, refine the selection with the Refine Selection Brush until it meets your needs.

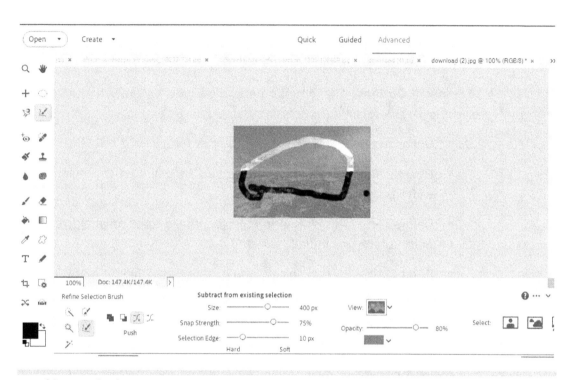

Working With The Cookie Cutter Tools

The Cookie Cutter tool is used to crop away or remove anything crooked in the image. To crop a picture into the desired shape, use the Cookie Cutter tool, in other words. To get your desired outcome, you may also utilize this tool to move or resize the bounding box.

Follow the procedure below to use the cookie-cutter tool.

To use the Cookie Cutter tool, follow the procedures below

- Go to the **Tools panel** and select **the Crop Tool**

- Go to the Tools panel and select the Crop Tool

- Then select the Cookie Cutter tool (The Cookie Cutter tool looks like a flower) from the Tools Option

- set the options you want in the Tool Options; these options are highlighted below

  - **Shape:** This allows you to select a shape from the Custom Shape picker preset library. To see other libraries, click on the Shape pop-menu and then select any of the submenus

  - **Geometry Options**: The options here allow you to draw a shape with specific parameters.

    - Unconstrained: This allows you to draw freely

    - Defined Proportions: This allows you to maintain the height and width proportional

    - Defined Size: This is used to crop the image to its original fixed size of the shape you initially selected.

    - Fixed Size: With this option, you can input the height and width of your choice

  - From Center: This feature enables you to draw the shape from the center

  - Feather: With this option, you can create a soft-edged selection

  - Crop: You can crop or cut an image to shape by using the Crop option

- You can now drag the mouse on the image to form the shape you want.

- Drag one of the handles of the bounding box to adjust the size of the shape.

- Then click on Enter to finish or use the comment button

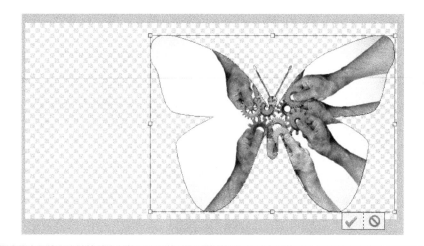

Working With Eraser Tools

The Eraser capabilities in the Photoshop Element cannot be overlooked among the other tools. The image can be completely erased using the Eraser tools. Three categories comprise the Eraser tools.

- ◆ The Regular Eraser tool
- ◆ The Magic Eraser Tool
- ◆ The Background Eraser Tool

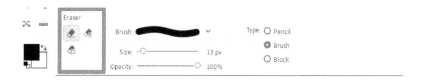

The Eraser Tool

You can erase your image to the backdrop color with the Eraser Tool. Follow these procedures to utilize the Eraser

- ◆ Go to the **Tools** panel and click on the **Eraser** tool button

- ◆ Choose the color you want as the background from the **Toolbox**

- ◆ Select the layer you want from the **Layer** option

- ◆ From the **Brush Preset Picker** menu, make a selection on the type of eraser you desire

- ◆ Set the width of the eraser tip from the **Size** slider

- Select the best brush option from the **Type** option

- To set the transparency level of the color, use the **Opacity** slider

- To erase by using the current settings, you can click and drag the image and apply it to the current background color

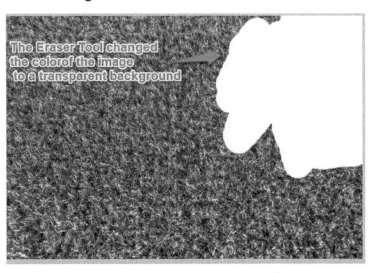

The Background Eraser

You can get rid of or erase the backdrop by using the Background Eraser tool. The foreground and the things on it are not touched by this tool. This utility removes the transparency backdrop from a layer. Additionally, the tool layers photos with just a background.

Follow the procedures below to utilize this tool

- Go to the **Tools** panel and click on the **Eraser** tool button

- Select the **Background Eraser Tool** in the **Tools Option**

- Use the **Layer** panel to select the layer on which to erase

- you can set the following options in the Background Eraser Options

  o **Brush Settings:** Here you get to set the brush tip options such as Size, Hardness, Spacing, Roundness, and Angle.

  o **Limits:** Here in this option, you can choose either Discontiguous or Contiguous. Discontiguous removes all similarly colored pixels anywhere they appear in the image, while Contiguous removes all similarly colored pixels that are together with the ones under the hot spot.

- o **Tolerance**: This option allows you to set the percentage that determines how identical the colors have to be with the color under the hot spot before it is deleted by the Photoshop Element

✦ The selected area disappears as you select the area you desire to erase.

The Magic Eraser Tool

If two adjacent pixels in an image need to be changed, utilize the Magic Eraser tool. When using this tool on a background layer or a layer with locked transparency, which prevents you from editing the transparent pixels, the transparent pixels will either change the background color or be erased to transparency. Contiguous pixels or pixels with comparable colors are the only pixels that can be erased using this tool. With photographs where the backdrop color differs from the subject, the Magic Eraser tool works well.

To use the Magic Eraser Tool, follow the steps below

✦ Go to **Tools Options** and click on the **Magic Eraser** tool button after selecting The Eraser Tool.

✦ Set the following options in the **Background Eraser** Options

- o **Sample All Layers:** This allows you to sample colors to erase by using the combined data of all visible layers as desired.

- o **Opacity:** This allows you to adjust the opacity of the erased pixels using the Opacity slider. When the opacity is at 100%, the selected pixels are completely erased, and a lower opacity partially deletes the pixels.

- o **Anti-aliasing:** This is used to create a selection that has smooth edges in the transparent area.

- o **Contiguous:** This allows you to erase all identical colored pixels that are together with the ones under the hot spot.

✦ After you have set the settings in the Tool Options, click into the image on the pixel color in the part of the image or layer to erase.

Using The Select Menu

We will navigate the Select menu in this session to learn how to perform a few actions on the Selections. Let's check what the Select menu can be used for now.

NOTE: The Select menu may be found in the menu on the Home Screen top. The submenu will appear when you select the Select menu, as seen in the illustration below.

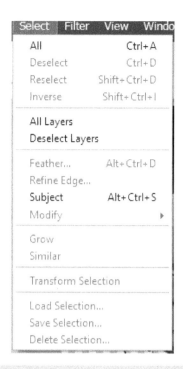

Selecting All Or Deselect All

✦ To select all the objects in an image, go to **Select** and click on **All** or use **Ctrl + A**

✦ To deselect all items in your image, go to Select and click on **Deselect**

Reselecting A Selection

✦ To restore your last selection, go to **Select** and click on **Reselect**

Inversing A Selection

✦ To use the Inverse selection for your image, go to **Select** and click on **Inverse**

Feathering A Selection

✦ To feather a selection, go to **Select**, input the desired number ranging from 0.2 to 250 pixels

Saving And Loading Selection

You can return to a selection you've saved for future use by doing so.

To save a selection, follow the steps below

- ✦ Go to **Select** and click Save Selection

- ✦ In the **Save Selection** dialog box that pops up, set the selection to **New Selection** and then type in the name of your selection in the **Name box**

- ✦ Then click on **Ok**

- ✦ After you have done this, you can go back to load the saved selection by going to **Select** and clicking on **Load Selection**, then choose from the Selection drop-down menu #

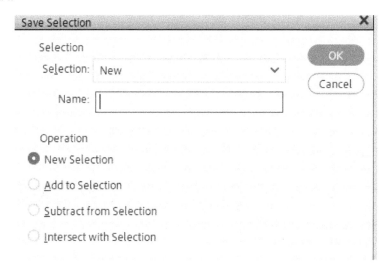

Refining The Edges Of A Selection

The Refine Edges allow you to fine-tune the edges of the selections made in your image. The Refine Edge can be found in tools such as **Lasso, Magic Wand, and Quick Selection tools.** To locate the Refine Edge

- ✦ Go to the **Select** menu and click on **Refine Edge** in the submenu dropdown

The following options can be seen in the Refine Edge

✦ **View Mode:** This allows you to choose a mode in the View pop-up menu. In the View mode, we have Marching Ants, Overlay, On Black and On White, and Original

✦ **Smart Radius:** This option allows you to correct or change the radius to have soft and hard-edge seen in the border region.

✦ **Radius:** This option is used to determine the size of the selection border where refinement takes place. The small radius is used for sharp edges while the larger one is for hard edges.

✦ **Smooth:** This is used to reduce rough edges in the selection border to have a smooth

✦ **Feather**: This is used to blur the shift between the selection and the pixels. To create a progressively softer and more blurred edge, move the slider to the right

✦ **Contrast:** When you increase the contrast, the soft-edged transition also increases around the selection border

- **Shift Edge**: This option is used to decrease or increase the selected portion in the image. When the selection border is decreased faintly, unwanted background colors are removed from the selection.

- **Decontaminate Colors:** This replaces the color fringe with the colors of the elements you have selected. The strength of the color replacement is relative to the softness of the edges selected.

- **Amount:** This is used to change the level of decontamination and that of fringe replacement.

- **Output To** This is used to determine if the refined edge turns into a selection or mask on the current layer, or produces a new layer or document.

- **Refine Radius Tool**: This is used to select the Paint Brush which is used to make corrections on the border you are working on while refining.

- **Erasement Refinement Tool**: This tool is used to remove any unwanted refinements that have been made, and it is located on the left-hand side.

- **Zoom Tool**: This is used to zoom your image to check the effect of the adjustments made in your settings

- **Hand Tool:** This allows you to move around your image to check the adjustments made in the settings

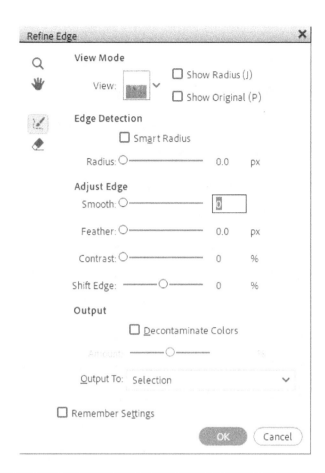

Working With The Modify Commands

Let's talk about the Modify commands located in the Select sub-menu. The Modify commands may not necessarily be important, but you never can tell where they can be of help. Briefly, we will just take a look at the modified commands

- ✦ **Border:** This command allows you to select an area ranging from 1 to 200 pixels, within the edge of the selection border

- ✦ **Smooth:** This command helps you to take away any rough edge by entering a value ranging from 1 to 100 pixels.

- ✦ **Expand:** With this command, you can increase the size of your selection by entering a value of pixels, ranging from 1 to 100.

- ✦ **Contract:** This command is the opposite of the Expand command. This command helps to decrease your selection border by 1 to 100 pixels.

CHAPTER TEN

WORKING WITH LAYERS

In this chapter, layers will receive a lot of attention, and we'll delve deeply into how layers can be utilized, as well as the tools and methods required to deal with levels.

Remember that layers provide you the freedom to alter as much as you want without limitations. Let's examine the layers now.

Getting To Know Layer

Layers, which are essentially digitalized versions of clear acetate sheets, let you edit and add to images while keeping the original intact. You can do the same operations on layers that you can on photos, such as modifying color and brightness, adding special effects, moving layer contents, defining opacity, blending values, etc. In addition, layers can be added, removed, hidden, and rearranged. The layer panel contains the layers.

The Overview of The Layer Panel

The Layers panel displays a list of each layer in the image, from top to bottom and from foreground to background. Go to **Windows** and select **Layers** to find the layer panel.

Let's now examine each item in the **layer** panel as depicted in the below image.

1. **Create New Layer:** This can be used to add a new layer to the available stack of layers and is found at the top of the layer panel. To add a new layer to the stack, you may also choose **Layer, New** from the menu, and then click **Layer**.
2. **Create a New Group:** By using this option, you can aggregate a sizable number of layers together.
3. **Fill/Adjustment Layer:** This makes it possible for you to add patterns, gradients, and colors to a layer. Additionally, you can adjust the levels, hue, saturation, and brightness with this option.
4. **Add Layer Mask:** You can reveal or hide a specific portion of a layer with the layer mask. Any portion of the mask that is hidden within the layer is presented in black, while the viewable portion of the mask is displayed in white. Additionally, for the thumbnails, pixels are hidden in black while exposed in white.
5. **Lock All Pixels:** You can lock all layers from being edited by clicking on this button.

6. **Lock Transparent Pixels:** Every layer in this option is taken into consideration to be transparent if it contains no image pixels. Additionally, no transparent layers can be edited.
7. **Delete Layer:** As its name implies, It allows you to delete any selected layer from the layer stack.
8. **Panel Options:** This contains a certain number of menu options such as Rename Layer, Duplicate Layer, Delete Layer, Link Layers, Merge Visible and Merge Down
9. **Blend Modes:** This option sets how image colors on the layer work together with the layer below.
10. **Visibility:** You can disable a layer's visibility by clicking on the tiny eye icon that can be seen on the left side of each layer. Remember that until you click on the eye icon, any alteration about this layer is also concealed.
11. **Link/Unlink Layers:** This is the option in the layer panel that links several layers together, in such a way that any transformation made to one affects all.
12. **Background:** The backdrop layer is the lowest layer by default. Whether you open a picture or a new document, the background layer is always partially frozen.

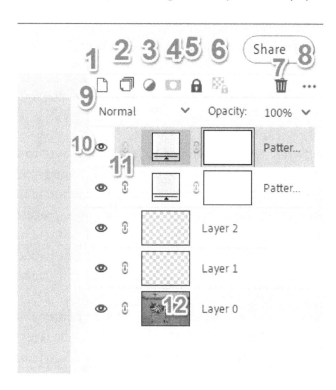

13. **Standard Layer:** This layer displays the pixel information for that layer.

167

14. **Adjustment Layer:** This layer was designed to have an impact on the layer beneath it.
15. **Vector Layer:** This layer holds scalable data, such as shapes.
16. **Text Layer:** The layer can now receive texts inside of it thanks to this setting. This layer's thumbnail is shown as a T.

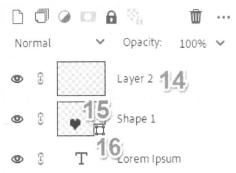

Working With The Layer Menu

Some commands can be used in both the Layer menu and the Layer panels. Go to the menu bar and select the Layer menu to access the Layer menu.

✦ **Deleted Linked Layers And Hidden layers:** These commands allow you to delete the layers that are linked or the layers that are hidden from display.

✦ **Layer Style:** This is the command responsible for supervising or handling the styles and special effects that are applied to the layers

✦ **Arrange:** With this command, you can arrange your layer stacking order using options such as Back to Front and Send to Back.

✦ **Create Clipping Mask**: This option allows you to create a clipping mask, where the bottommost layer acts as a mask for the layer above it. The clipping mask is best used when you intend to fill a shape or type with different image layers.

✦ **Type**: This command helps to manage the display of type layers.

✦ **Rename**: With this command, you can rename the layer, giving it a new name

✦ **Simplify Layer:** This is the command that converts a type layer, shape layer, or fills layer into a normal image layer.

- ♦ **Merge And Flatten:** These commands join a variety of layers together and then make them a single layer. In the case of flattening, it joins all layers into a single background.

- ♦ **Panel Options:** When selected, you can display options and also use the layer mask on the adjustments layers.

Working With Different Layers Types

There are 5 kinds of layers in Photoshop Element, and here in this chapter, we will be learning more about them, but know this, of all the layers in Element, you will have to spend more time creating the image layers.

The Image Layers

The Image Layer is the original photographs and any image that is imported into the document to occupy an Image layer. To create a new layer, follow the steps below

- ♦ Go to **Window** and click on **Layers** for the **Layers panel** to display

- ♦ Double-click on **Background** in the **Layer panel**

- ♦ Enter the name of the layer or leave it a default name

- ♦ Then press **Ok**

The Adjustment Layer

These layers are used to adjust an image's brightness, contrast, and saturation.

Follow these procedures to use the Adjustment layers.

- Go to **Window** and click on **Layers** for the **Layers panel** to display

- Select the Image you want to work on

- **In the Layers panel**, click **Create New Fill or Adjustment Layers,**

- From the drop-down list, set the following options for the Adjustment layers

  o **Level:** This adjusts the tonal value in the image

  o **Brightness/Contrast**: This option either lightens or darkens the image

  o **Hue/Saturation**: This option helps to correct a color deficiency in the image

  o **Gradient Map:** This option locates the pixels to the color in the gradient selected.

  o **Photo Filter:** This option helps to correct the color balance and color temperature of the image

  o **Invert:** This is used to create a photo with a negative effect by creating negativity based on the brightness values of the image

  o **Threshold:** This is used to create an image in monochrome with no gray so that you can find the lightest and darkest area of the image.

  o **Posterize:** This option reduces the number of brightness values in the image by giving you a flat, poste-like appearance to your picture. When you use this option, the number of colors is reduced.

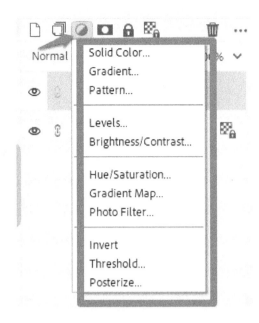

- Then click on **Ok.**

It is important to know that you automatically create a layer mask anytime an Adjustment is created.

The Fill layers

You can add a solid color, gradient, or pattern to an image using the fill layers. The fill layers have layer masks much as the adjustment layers do.

Follow the procedures listed below to build a fill layer.

- Open the image you want to work on

- **In the Layers panel,** click **Create New Fill or Adjustment Layers.**

- From the drop-down list, set the following options

  - **Solid Color**: This is where you choose the color to add to the layer

  - **Gradient**: This permits you to apply the gradient to your layer by selecting a preset gradient from the drop-down panel

  - **Pattern:** You get to select a pattern from the drop-down panel. You can also input a value to scale the pattern of the layer.

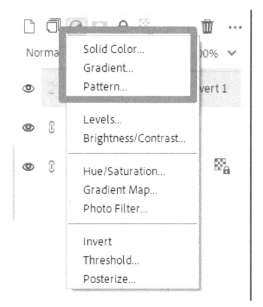

- Then click on **Ok.**

The Shape Layer

The Shape layers assist in adding various shapes to an image. These forms can be scaled and even given smooth edges. Follow these steps to utilize the form layers:

- Select the **Shape** tools in the **Tool** panel
- Pick any shape of your choice from the **Tool Option**.
- Click and drag the shape on the image to draw a shape

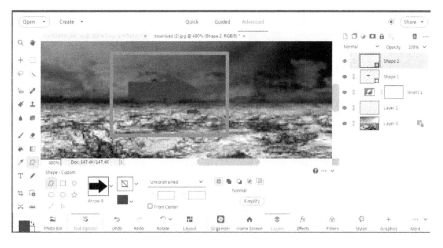

- If you have a layer selected, the shape will be placed into the layer and if not, a new layer will be created automatically.

The Text Layers

You can incorporate words into your photographs using these layers. By default, the text in the Photoshop Element is vector-based, which implies that you can alter and resize the text as you add it.

- Select the Text tool from the Tool Panel
- Click into a layer and begin to type the text you want
- When you are done, click on the marker icon.

- The Text will appear on a blank layer if you have the blank layer selected as shown in the image below.

Dealing With Layers Basics

We will learn different methods for producing image layers in this section of the chapter as we deal more with picture layers.

Creating A New Layer From Scratch

There are two primary ways to create layers in the Photoshop Element, and they are as follows:

The First Method:

❖ Click on **Create a new layer** on the **Layers panel** and the layer will be created automatically giving it a default name; **layer 1**

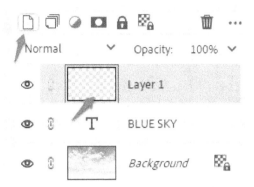

The Second Method:

❖ Click on **Layer** in the Menu bar
❖ Select **New** and click on **Layer**

❖ In the **New Layer** dialog box, set the options given below

    o **Name**: Enter the name of the new layer

    o **Color**: Set the color you wish to apply

    o **Mode**: Set the mode in the Mode drop-down list

    o Opacity: Use the Opacity slider to set the layer opacity.

✦ Then click on **OK** and the new layer will be displayed as a thumbnail on the left-hand side in the layer panel.

Using Layer Via Copy And Layer Via Cut

Using the Layer via copy and Layer via cut in the layer menu command, you can create a new layer

✦ Click on Layer from the menu bar
✦ Select **New** and click on **Layer Via Copy** or **Layer Via Cut.**

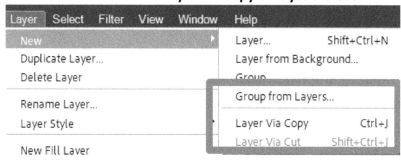

Duplicating Layers

Your layers can be duplicated as frequently as you wish in many copies. Use the instructions below to duplicate layers.

✦ After selecting **Layer** from the menu bar, click on the **Duplicate layer.**

✦ In the **Duplicate layer** dialog box, set the options given and then click on **Ok**

Dragging And Dropping Layers

You can use the drag and drop command to duplicate a layer rather than the copy and paste method. Follow these procedures to accomplish this.

- Select the layer you want to move in the **Layer panel**
- Go to the **Tool** panel and select the **Move** tool
- Drag and drop to where you want it to be

Transforming Layer

The Transform and Free Transform commands can be used to rotate or scale your photos as part of layer transformations.

the methods listed here to transform a layer

- Select the layer you wish to transform
- Go to **Image,** select **Transform**, and then click **Free Transform**
- Here, your layer is surrounded by a bounding box
- Adjust the bounding box by setting the following options
  - **Size the contents**: To do this, drag the corner handle
  - **Constrain the proportions**: Use the Shift key while dragging
  - **Rotate the content**: To rotate the content, move the mouse cursor outside the corner handle and wait until changes to a curved arrow, and then drag
  - **Distort, skew, or apply perspective to the contents**: To execute these options, right-click and select the command you want from the context

menu. You can also locate the scale and skew icons in the Tools Option, even by entering the transform values numerically.

✦ When the layer is transformed to what you want, double-click inside the bounding box

Working With The layer Mask

The visibility of a layer that is added to the image is managed and controlled by the layer mask, which is a resolution-dependent bitmap image. A part of a picture can be shown or hidden using the layer mask. Any portion of the mask that is hidden within the layer is presented in black, while the viewable portion of the mask is displayed in white.

Without increasing or decreasing the masked area, the layer mask can be modified without erasing any layer pixels.

The layer mask can be used for the following things.

✦ To add one layer to another

✦ To adjust the layer mask to either show or hide the effects of the adjustment layer.

Adding The Layer Mask To An Image

Select the area of the image you want to use the layer mask on, and then click the **Add Layer Mask button** in the **Layer panel.**

Other Operations On The Layer Masks

These are some things you can perform with layer masks.

✦ Shift-click a layer mask thumbnail in the Layers panel to make it invisible.

- Alt-click the layer mask thumbnail in the Layers panel to reveal the mask without displaying the image.
- Click the link icon in the Layer panel to break a layer's link to a layer mask.
- Drag the layer mask thumbnail to the trash icon in the Layers panel to delete a layer mask.

Flattening The Layers

To flatten the layers, the hidden layers must be removed, and the visible region must be filled with white. Reducing the file size is another step in flattening the layer. When an image is flattened, all of the layers: the visible layers text, shape, fill, and adjustment layers—are combined into a Background.

To use the Flatten option, do the following

- Ensure that the layers to be flattened are visible

- Go to the **Layer menu** and then click on **Flatten Image**

Merging The Layers

All of the layers can be combined into a single Background with the use of file merging. This combines visible, linked, or neighboring levels into one layer and helps save memory and storage space.

To merge layers, do the following

- Select all layers to be merged

- From the **Menu bar**, go to **Layer** and then click on **Merge Layers**

CHAPTER ELEVEN

SIMPLE IMAGE MAKEOVER

You will learn how to crop, straighten, and recompose photographs with ease in this chapter. Additionally, with step-by-step guidance, you will become familiar with the Auto repairs, including Auto Smart Tone, Auto Smart Fix, Auto Levels, Auto contrast, etc.

Cropping Images

Among the most crucial picture editing techniques you should master is cropping images. To create a strong focus point and get rid of distracting backgrounds, crop an image. The quickest and easiest way to crop an image is to use the Crop tool.

Cropping With The Crop Tool

To use the Crop tool, follow the steps below

- Go to the **Tools panel** and click on the **Crop tool**

- Indicate the aspect ratio and resolution options in the Tool Options provided

    o **No Restriction**: This enables you to cut your image to any size

    o **Use Photo Ratio**: This helps to preserve the original aspect of the image when cropping

    o **Preset Sizes**: This gives you several options of the common photographic sizes

    o **Width (W) and Height (H)**: This allows you to choose the width and height you want to crop an image.

    o **Resolution**: This allows you to choose the resolution you want for your cropped image.

    o **Pixels/ins Pixel/cm**: Here you choose the measurement of units you want

    o **Grid Overlay**: This helps to frame your image before cropping. This option has three parts; None, Grid, and Rule of Thirds.

- Drag over the part of the image you wish to keep, and then release the mouse when the crop marquee displays as a bounding box with handles at the corners and size.

✦ Then click on the green Commit button

Cropping With A Selection Borders

The selection border can also be used to crop an image. The region outside the selection boundary is eliminated when a picture is cropped with a selection border. The procedures shown below can be used to crop an image using a chosen border.

✦ From the **Tool panel**, choose the **Straighten tool.**

✦ Choose the settings you want from the **Canvas Options** in the **Tools Option**

   ○ **Grow or Shrink:** This option allows you to rotate the image and either decrease or increase the size of the canvas to fit the image area.

      ○ **Remove Background**: you can shape the background canvas out of the image.

      ○ **Original Size**: This rotates the image without shaping the background canvas.

✦ Draw a line to your image specifying the new straight edge

Recomposing images

You can resize your image with the Recompose tool without sacrificing any significant objects or content. the procedures listed below to use the Recompose tool;

✦ From the **Tool panel**, choose the **Recompose tool**

✦ Use the **Mark for Protection Brush (the brush with a plus sign)** in the **Tool Options**, and then brush over the area of the image you wish to retain

- Use the **Mark for Protection Brush (the brush with a minus sign)** in the **Tool Options**, and then brush over the area of the image you wish to remove

- Set any of the settings in the **Tool Options**

  o **Threshold:** The Threshold slider is used to set how much recomposing displays in the adjustment.

  o **Preset Ratios:** This is the option that allows you to frame your image into dimensions.

  o **Width and Height:** This is where you resize any image to a specified dimension.

  o **Highlight Skin Tones:** This option disallows the skin tones from altering when resizing.

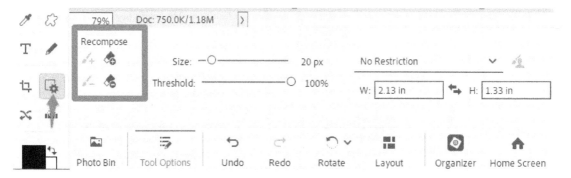

- Drag the corner or side handles to resize or recompose

- Finally, click on the **Commit button** after you have completed the editing.

Introducing One-Step The Auto Fixes

The Auto Fixes are useful tools for quickly adjusting lighting, contrast, and color to improve the photo's appearance with a single menu command. In both Advanced and Quick mode, these commands are available on the Enhance menu.

Auto Smart Fix

A potent tool for making quick adjustments to frequent issues like contrast, color balance, and saturation is the Auto Smart Fix.

The graphic below displays the Auto Smart Fix's before-and-after results.

Auto Smart Tone

To alter the tonal values in your photograph, the Auto Smart Tone auto fix was developed.

- When your image is open, select **Enhance** and then click **Auto Smart Tone**.
- To perfect the adjustment, move the controller to the center of the image.
- In the dialog box's lower-left corner, click the **Learn from This Correction option**.
- After making the necessary modifications, click **OK**.

Auto level

The Auto Level adjusts an image's hue as well as its overall contrast. This function makes the darkest portion of the image darker and the lightest area lighter by converting the image's lightest and darkest pixels to black and white. The image below displays the Auto Levels' before-and-after results.

Auto Contrast

The Auto Contrast function is used to adjust an image's contrast without altering its color. With hazy photos, this works best. The image below displays the Auto Contrast's before-and-after results.

Auto Haze Removal

Your photos can be cleared of haze and fog with the help of Auto Haze Removal. If this command does not satisfy you, you may want to look at the Haze Removal tool in the Tools panel. The following image contrasts the Auto Haze Removal's results before and after.

Auto Color Correction

An image's color and contrast that is focused on the shadows, highlights, and mid-tones can be improved with the help of Auto Color Correction. This command can also be used to balance the color in your image or eliminate a cast color. Below is a comparison of the image with and without the use of Auto Color Correction.

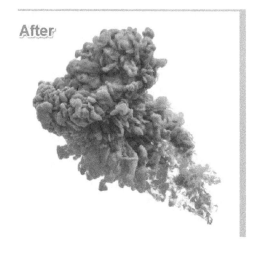

Auto Shake Reduction

To lessen the blur caused by camera movement, Auto Shake Reduction was developed. When necessary, this command is useful. Go to Enhance and select Shake Reduction for additional Shake Reduction enjoyment. The following image displays the Auto Shake before and after.

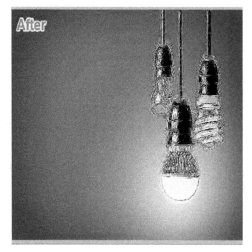

Auto Sharpen

The Auto Sharpen command aids in enhancing pixel contrast, which sharpens the image's focus. An image that has been too sharpened appears noisy and grainy.

Auto Red-Eye Fix

Red-eye in an image can be found and fixed with the Auto Red Fix command. When a person or animal looks straight into the flash, a red-eye happens. You can utilize the Red Eye tool in the Tools menu if the Auto Red Eye feature is ineffective.

 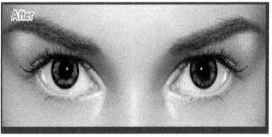

CHAPTER TWELVE

CORRECTING CONTRAST, COLOR, AND CLARITY

In this chapter, we'll focus on applying manual fixes to enhance contrast, color, and clarity in your images when quick and simple fixes fall short of your expectations.

Adjusting Color

One of the goals that every Element user has is to change the colors of their image. You will also learn the manual instructions used to change the colors of photos in this section of the guide.

Removing Colors Cast Automatically

When the color channels in the image are out of balance, a color cast results. The undesirable appearance, which frequently takes the form of an odd color tint, is a frequent consequence of the image's poor lighting. One of the primary causes of color cast in photographs is fluorescence light. To balance the color in your photographs and get rid of the cast, the Remove Color Cast command was developed.

Follow these procedures to use the Remove Color Cast.

- ✦ Go to **Enhance** on the menu bar, select **Adjust Color,** and then click on **Remove Color Cast.**

Adjusting Lighting

To improve the lighting in pictures, many straightforward techniques may be used in place of auto repairs. Most crucially, the Advanced and Quick modes contain these manual fixes. Let's now examine them.

Fixing Lighting With Shadows/Highlights

Using the Shadows/Highlights commands, you may quickly and easily adjust overexposed and underexposed sections in your photographs. This command works nicely with photos that were taken overhead or in harsh lighting. Follow these procedures to use this command.

- ✦ Select **Adjust Lighting** from the menu bar's **Enhance** section, then choose **Shadows/Highlight**. Select the **Preview** check box after that.

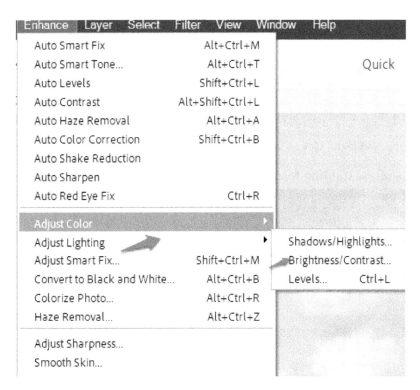

To change the level of brightness and contrast correction, drag the sliders or enter a value in the **Brightness and Contrast** dialog box.

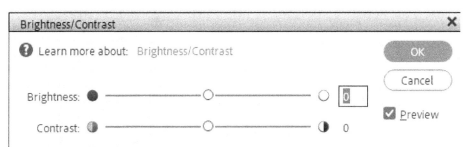

Click on **OK when** you are done with the adjustment.

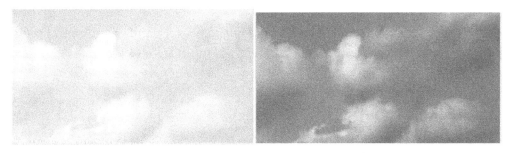

Using The Levels

You have precise control over the outcome with the Level command. In comparison to the Brightness/Contrast command, levels allow you to change up to 256 different tones and produce a far more natural-looking finished product.

Follow these instructions to use Levels.

- ✦ Select **Adjust Lighting** from the menu bar's **Enhance** section, followed by **Levels**. Select the **Preview** check box after that.

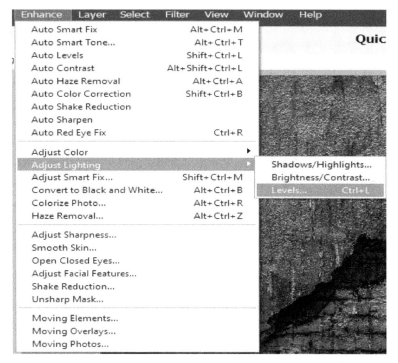

- ✦ Select **RGB** from the **Channel menu**

- ✦ Set the shadow and highlight values by dragging the black and white **Input Levels sliders** or input the values into the first and third **Input Levels text boxes.**

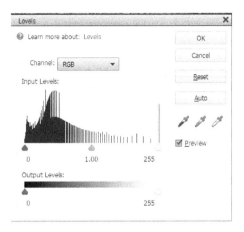

◆ Then click on **Ok**

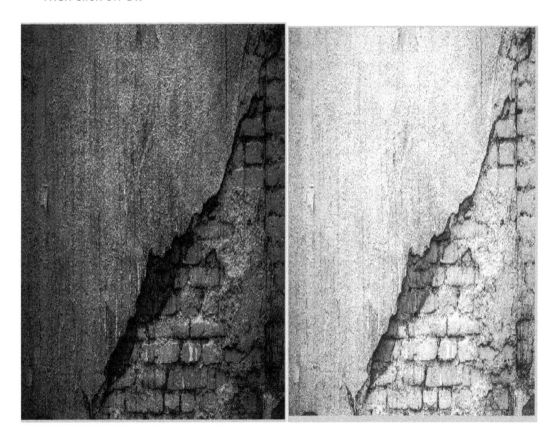

Adjusting Color

One of the goals that every Element user has is to change the colors of their image. You will also learn the manual instructions used to change the colors of photos in this section of the textbook.

Removing Colors Cast Automatically

When the color channels in the image are out of balance, a color cast results. The undesirable appearance, which frequently takes the form of an odd color tint, is a frequent consequence of the image's poor lighting. One of the primary causes of color cast in photographs is fluorescence light. To balance the color in your photographs and get rid of the cast, the Remove Color Cast command was developed.

Follow these procedures to use the Remove Color Cast.

✦ Go to **Enhance** on the menu bar, select **Adjust Color,** and then click on **Remove Color Cast**

✦ In the **Remove Color Cast** dialog box, the command works when you click the **Eyedropper** tool into the image where it should be white, gray, or black. With this information, the colors are fine-tuned accordingly.

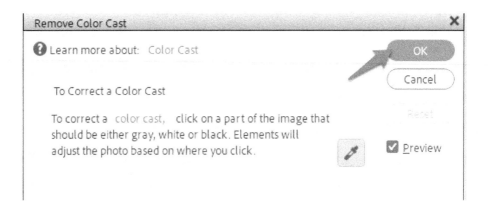

❖ To save the changes made, click on the **Ok** button.

Adjusting With Hue/Saturation

Your image's hue corresponds to the color, whilst its saturation corresponds to the color's strength. You can fine-tune or modify the color of your image with the Hue/Saturation command based on its hue, saturation, and lightness.

✦ Go to **Enhance** on the menu bar, select **Adjust Color,** and then click on **Adjust Hue/Saturation.**

✦ In the **Master** option, select any of the colors to adjust.

✦ Drag the slider of the following options to adjust the color

　　o **Hue:** This option moves the colors clockwise or counters-wise around the color wheel.

　　o **Saturation:** This option increases or decreases the richness of the colors

　　o **Lightness:** This increases the brightness values by adding white or decreases the brightness value by adding black.

✦ Select the **Colorize** option to change the colors in the image to either new or single color.

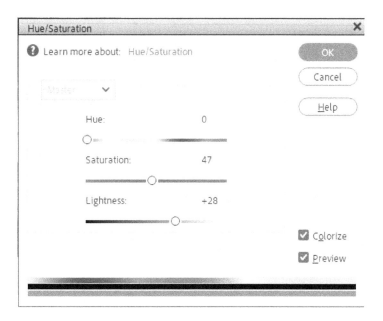

✦ Click **Ok** after making the necessary adjustments.

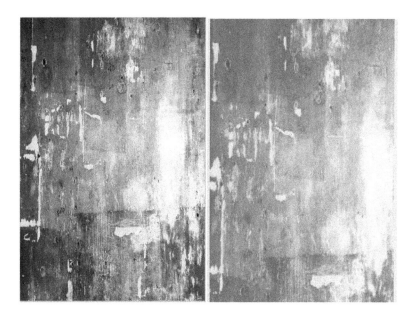

Eliminating Color With Remove Color

If you wish to easily remove color from any picture, layer, or selection, Element provides a straightforward method for doing so. Using the Remove Color command might occasionally result in a low-contrast image. To employ the command "Remove Color".

✦ Select the image, layer, or selection you wish to remove the color

✦ Go to **Enhance** on the menu bar, select **Adjust Color,** and then click on **Remove Color.**

Switching Colors With Replace Color

You can change a color in your image by using the Replace Color command. To use this command, you must first construct a mask (see the last chapter for instructions on how to do this) and then precisely adjust the hue and saturation of the colors you've chosen to get the desired effect. Follow these steps to utilize the Replace Color command:

✦ Go to **Enhance** on the menu bar, select **Adjust Color,** and then click on **Replace Color.**

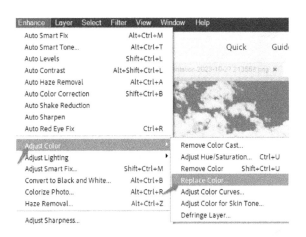

- In the **Replace Color** dialog box, select either **Selection** or **Image; Selection** reveals the mask in the **Preview** area while **Image** reveals the real image in the **Preview** area

- Ensure to choose the color you desire in the image or Preview area.

- To add more colors, use the Shift-click or the plus sign (+) Eyedropper tool

- To delete colors, press the Alt key or use the minus sign (-) Eyedropper tool

- Use the **Fuzziness** slider, to add colors related to the ones you have selected. You can also use the Fuzziness slider to fine-tune, add, or delete your selection.

- To change the color, use the **Hue slider**. To change the color richness, use the **Saturation slider**. To lighten or darken your image, use the **Lightness slider.**

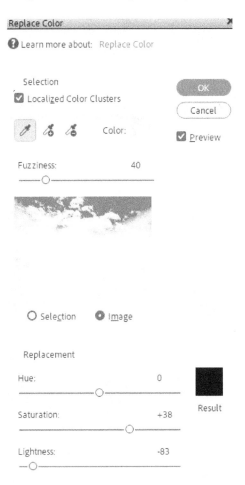

❖ Click on **Ok** when you are done with making the necessary adjustments.

Correcting With Color Curves

By adjusting the highlights, shadows, and mid-tones in each color channel, the Color Curves command aims to increase the overall tonal range in color photographs. Images that are overexposed or have a dark backlight are the ideal candidates for this command. How to operate the Color Curves command.

❖ Go to **Enhance** on the menu bar, select **Adjust Color,** and then click on **Adjust Color Curves.**

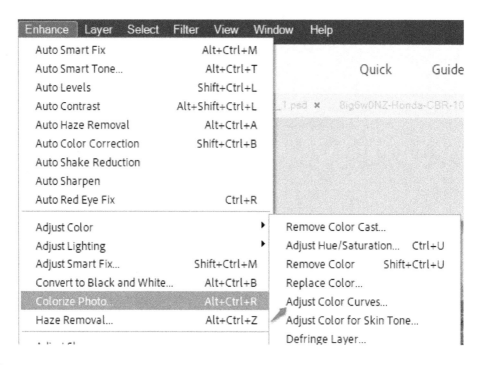

❖ In the **Adjust Color Curves**, select the curve adjustment styles from the **Select a Style** area

- Use the highlights, brightness, contrast, and shadow adjustment sliders for better fine-tuning.

- Click on **Ok** when the adjustment is up to your satisfaction.

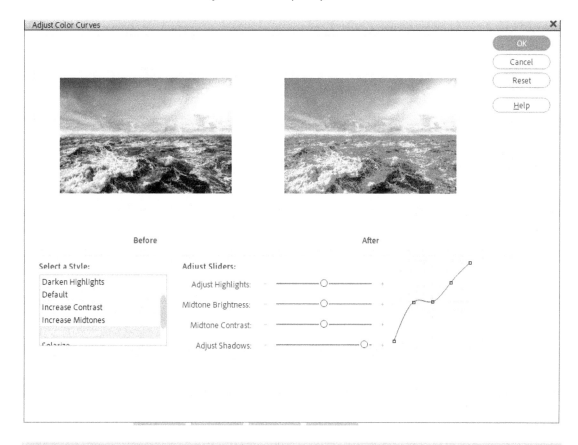

Adjusting Skin Tones

Poor-looking skin tones can be caused by a variety of things in your photos or people. To assist the skin tone in returning to a more natural appearance, Elements provides the Adjust Skin Tones command. You can modify a selection or a whole layer using this command. You should use the selection tool to choose the area of the tool you wish to edit to change the portion of your image that you do not want to change. Follow these steps to utilize the Adjust Skin Tones command:

- Select the layer or area of the skin that is to be adjusted

- Go to **Enhance** on the menu bar, select **Adjust Color,** and then click on **Adjust Skin Tone.**

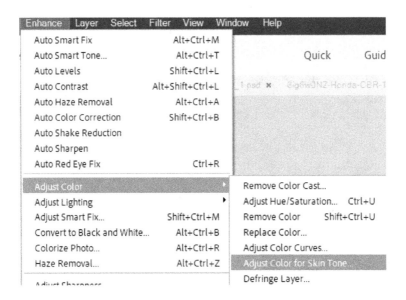

♦ Click on the part of the skin that needs to be adjusted

♦ Set the following options

- o **Tan**: To remove or add the volume of brown in the skin amount

- o **Brush**: To remove or add the volume of red in the skin

- o **Temperature:** To adjust the overall color of the skin, causing it to be warmer (right toward red) or cooler (left toward blue)

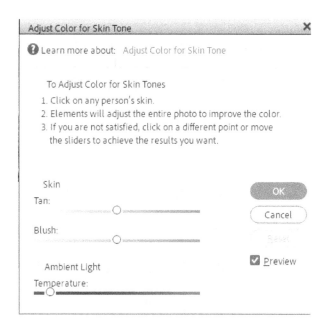

Adjust Color for Skin Tone ✕

ⓘ Learn more about: Adjust Color for Skin Tone

To Adjust Color for Skin Tones
1. Click on any person's skin.
2. Elements will adjust the entire photo to improve the color.
3. If you are not satisfied, click on a different point or move the sliders to achieve the results you want.

Skin
Tan:

Blush:

OK
Cancel
Reset

Ambient Light
Temperature:

☑ Preview

✦ When you are done with the adjustments, click on **Ok**

Defringing layers

The term "fringe" refers to the area that is frequently encountered when a selection is made, moved, or copied. The group of background pixels that surround your selection is known as the fringe. When the Defringed layers command is applied, the colors of these

202

unneeded extra pixels are altered to match the colors of nearby pixels that do not make up the background color.

Follow these procedures to utilize the Defringed Layers command.

✦ Drag and drop the selection into a new document or you can copy and paste a selection into a new or existing layer

✦ Go to **Enhance** on the menu bar, select **Adjust Color,** and then click on **Defringing Layers**

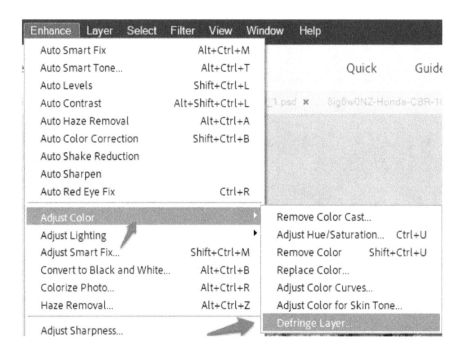

✦ Input the value for the number of pixels you desire to convert.

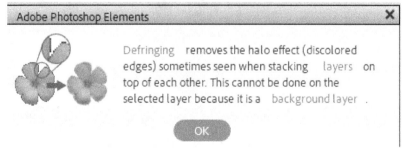

✦ After making the necessary adjustments, click on **OK**

Eliminating Haze

To manually remove hazes and fog from your image, use the Haze Removal tool. Light interacting with airborne dust, dirt, or other particles can produce haze or fog.

Follow the instructions listed below to use the Haze Removal Tools.

- Select the image that is to be adjusted

- Go to **Enhance** on the menu bar and select **Haze Removal**

- **In the Haze Removal** dialog box, set the following options

    o **Haze Reduction:** This slider allows you to adjust the volume of hazes in the image

    o **Sensitivity:** This slider is used to adjust how sensitive the images are to the Haze Removal

    o **Before and After Toggle Button:** This is used to switch between the before and after views of your image.

- When you are done with the adjustments, click on **Ok**

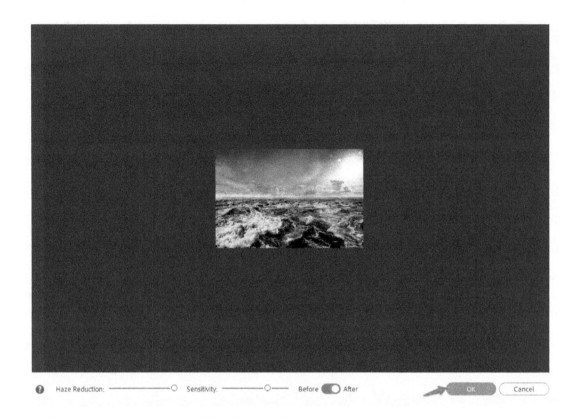

Haze Reduction: ──────○── Sensitivity: ──────○── Before ●○ After   OK   Cancel

Adjusting Color Temperature With Photo Filter

Using the Photo Filter Adjustment command, you can modify the color temperature in your image. Follow these procedures to use this command.

- From the **Filter** Menu, select **Adjustment** and click on **Photo Filter**.
- Choose the Preset filter from the drop-down list under Filter in the dialog box.
- Set the volume of color to apply to your image under the **Density option**.
- Click on **Preserve Luminosity** to prevent the photo filter from darkening your image.
- When all the modifications have been completed, click on **Ok**.

Mapping Your Colors

The color mapper commands make it easier to alter the color values in your image. Go to Filter and select Adjustments to find the color mapper command. The Adjustments submenu's commands for mapping colors are as follows:

- **Equalize:** This mapper looks for the lightest and darkest pixels in a picture and assigns white and black values to them. Grayscale values are assigned to the remaining pixels.
- **Gradient Map:** This matches the color of the gradient you select to the tonal range of an image. For instance, the shadow, highlight, and mid-tones are assigned to hues like orange, green, and purple.
- **Invert:** This flips all of the hues in your image, making them all negative.
- **Posterize:** This command assists in lowering your image's brightness levels. You can select a value between 2 and 255. Lower values produce images that resemble posters, while higher values produce more photorealistic images.
- **Threshold:** With this command, you can convert your image to black and white. All pixels that are brighter than the value you specify are displayed in white, while pixels that are darker than the value you specify are shown in black.

Adjusting Clarity

You only need to make your photographs' contrast and color adjustments. You must understand how to alter the quality of your photographs if you want to give them a professional appearance. As a result, we will discover various strategies for modifying your image's clarity.

Removing Noise, Artifacts, Dust, and Scratch

You might not get the results you want from your photograph because of noises, artifacts, dust, and scratches. You must go to **Filter** and select the **Noise section** to get rid of all these unwanted elements from your image. The Add Noise option is an exception to the Noise submenu's other choices, which are as follows:

- **Despeckle**: This option is responsible for decreasing the contrast, removing the dust in your image, and also leaving the edges unaffected.

- **Dust & Scratches:** This helps to apply blurs to your image to help hide the dust and scratches in your image. The Radius value in this option helps to set the size of the area you wish to blur. Also, the Threshold value in the option, when set, is used to determine the level of contrast between pixels that must be present before they are blurred.

- **Median:** This is used to decrease the contrast surrounding the dust spots. Ensure to set the radius value, which is the size of the area to be adjusted.

206

- **Reduce Noise:** This option is aimed at removing luminance noise and artifacts from your images. Your image becomes overly grainy with the luminance noise. To reduce the noise in your images, set the following options under Reduce noise.

  - **Strength:** This is used to specify the volume of noise reduction

  - **Preserve Details:** In this option, a higher percentage reserves the edges and details but decreases the amount of noise removed.

  - **Reduce Color Noise:** This is aimed at removing random colored pixels.

  - **Remove JPEG Artifact:** This is used to eradicate all the blocks and halos that are visible during the JPEG low-quality compression.

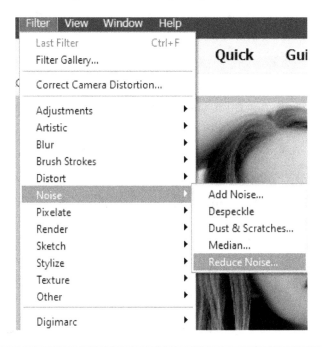

Blurring Your Image

By adjusting the pixel values, contrast, and sharpness, the blur tool is generally used to add a blur effect to images. You must blur your image when it is excessively grainy to solve this issue. To eliminate distractions or even to make the foreground appear clearer and serve as a focal point, you might need to blur the backdrop of your photograph.

Navigate to **Filter** and select the **Blur option** to access the blurring command.

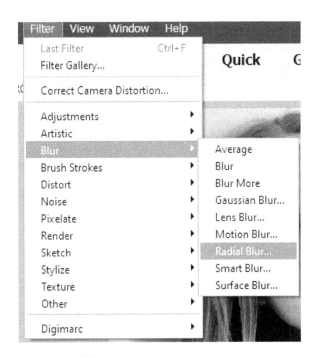

The Blurring commands are as follows:

- **Average:** This is a one-step filter that aids in determining the picture's average value and covers the region with that value. When you need to smooth out a section of your image that is too noisy, this is useful.
- **Blur:** Another one-step filter, this one similarly applies a fixed amount of burning to the entire image.
- **Blur More:** This is quite similar to blurring, yet it produces results that are superior to blur.
- **Gaussian Blur:** This is the most popular kind of blur because you can moderately regulate the kind and degree of blurring you get with it. This provides a Radius parameter that enables you to select the desired level of blur.
- **Motion Blur:** This kind of blur makes the blur of a moving item more noticeable so that the filter can be applied. In this case, you must define the blur's distance and motion angle.
- **Radical Blur:** This blur should be used to accentuate the blur on moving objects. This contributes to the circular blue effect.
- **Smart Blur:** This provides you with several options so you can decide how the blur should be applied. You will need to enter the radius and threshold values here. Additionally, you must choose the following mode:
  - **Normal:** This blurs the entire image or selection

- o **Edge Only:** This only blurs the edges of the images and uses black and white in the blurred pixels.

- o **Overlay Edge**: This also blurs the edges, but only applies white to the blurred pixels.

- **Surface Blur:** This ignores the boundaries and merely blurs the surface or interior of an image.
- **Lens Blur:** When a photo is taken using a camera, blurring is utilized, and this mimics that. Faster, blurry focus distance and invert are the three functions that come with this filter.

Sharpening For Better Focus

Another important aspect you must consider when working on your photographs is sharpening them. The primary goal of the sharpening tools is to improve the contrast between adjacent pixels. These are the two sharpening instructions that will be highlighted in this session:

- Unsharp Mask
- Adjust Sharpness

Unsharp Mask

The shot is sharpened using the Unsharp Mask filter. This method works well for printed images but is mostly demonstrated in images that are projected for on-screen projection. You might need to change the settings for printed photographs to improve the print quality.

To apply the Unsharp Mask,

- Go to the **Enhance menu** and click on **Adjust Sharpness**

Enhance	Layer	Select	Filter	View	V
Auto Smart Fix				Alt+Ctrl+M	
Auto Smart Tone...				Alt+Ctrl+T	
Auto Levels				Shift+Ctrl+L	
Auto Contrast				Alt+Shift+Ctrl+L	
Auto Haze Removal				Alt+Ctrl+A	
Auto Color Correction				Shift+Ctrl+B	
Auto Shake Reduction					
Auto Sharpen					
Auto Red Eye Fix				Ctrl+R	
Adjust Color					
Adjust Lighting					
Adjust Smart Fix...				Shift+Ctrl+M	
Convert to Black and White...				Alt+Ctrl+B	
Colorize Photo...				Alt+Ctrl+R	
Haze Removal...				Alt+Ctrl+Z	
Adjust Sharpness...					
Smooth Skin...					
Open Closed Eyes...					
Adjust Facial Features...					
Shake Reduction...					
Unsharp Mask...					
Moving Elements...					
Moving Overlays...					
Moving Photos...					

✦ In the **Adjust Sharpness** dialog box, mark the **Preview** checkbox and set the following options

- o Amount: This specifies the volume of the edge sharpening, ranging from 1 to 500. The higher the value, the more contrast between the edges.

- o **Radius**: This specifies the width (from 0 1 to 500) of the edges that the filter intends to sharpen.

- o **Preset**: This is where you save your sharpening settings and reload later.

- o **Remove**: This is where you choose your sharpening algorithm.

- o **Angle**: This is used to indicate the direction of motion for the Motion Blur algorithm.

- o **Shadows/Highlights:** This is where you control the volume of sharpening in sharpening in the Shadow and Highlights areas of your image.

- Then click on **Ok**

Open Closed Eyes

If the Element can identify the eyes inside a face, you can apply a set of chosen eyes to a face within an image using the open-closed eyes command. This makes it simple to adjust closed eyes within a photo and replicate a matched pair of eyes from one photo to another. The eye replacement works when the two images are more comparable.

Follow the instructions listed below to utilize the Open Closed Eyes command.

- Open the image you intend to use

- Go to the **Enhance menu** and click on **Open Closed Eyes**

- Click on the source image to apply it.

- When you are done, click on **Ok**

211

Enhance | Layer | Select | Filter | View | Wi

Auto Smart Fix	Alt+Ctrl+M
Auto Smart Tone...	Alt+Ctrl+T
Auto Levels	Shift+Ctrl+L
Auto Contrast	Alt+Shift+Ctrl+L
Auto Haze Removal	Alt+Ctrl+A
Auto Color Correction	Shift+Ctrl+B
Auto Shake Reduction	
Auto Sharpen	
Auto Red Eye Fix	Ctrl+R
Adjust Color	▶
Adjust Lighting	▶
Adjust Smart Fix....	Shift+Ctrl+M
Convert to Black and White...	Alt+Ctrl+B
Colorize Photo...	Alt+Ctrl+R
Haze Removal...	Alt+Ctrl+Z
Adjust Sharpness...	
Smooth Skin...	
Open Closed Eyes...	
Adjust Facial Features...	
Shake Reduction...	
Unsharp Mask...	

✦ In the **Open Closed Eyes** dialog box, a circle surrounds the affected area.

✦ Choose a photo as the eye source image, either from your computer or from your organizer.

Colorizing A Photo

With the Colorize Photo command, you can choose to manually colorize a specific area of the image or automatically colorize the entire image.

Use the Colorize Photo command by doing the actions listed below.

✦ Go to the **Enhance menu** and click on **Colorize Photo**

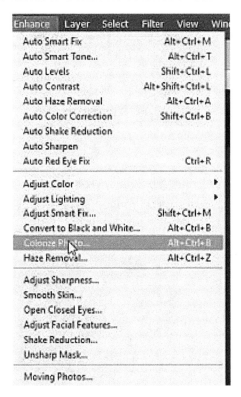

✦ In the **Colorize Photo** window, set the following options

- o **Zoom Tool:** This is used to zoom the image

- o **Hand Tool:** To pan in the images as needed.

- o **The Colorize panel:** This panel allows you to change your images to different colors.

- o **The Toggle Switch:** This allows you to move from the **Auto button** to the **Manual button**

213

✦ Click the toggle button and then set the following to manually colorize your photo:

- o Click on the **Selection tool** or the **Magic Wand** tool to choose the selection tool to use

- o **New**: This is used to make a new selection

- o **Add:** To add a new selection to an existing selection

- o **Subtract**: To subtract from an existing selection.

- o **Tolerance**: This is used to set the desired settings for the selection tool you choose.

- o **Droplet Tool**: This is used to add droplets to each color to droplets within the selection to mark the current color to colorize with a new color.

- o **Color palette**: To change the color of the selected area, use the color palette.

- o **All Application Colors**: You can also select a color from this option by using the sliders.

- o **Show Droplet**: This is used to toggle the appearance of the selections on and off as needed.

- o **Before and After** This is used to toggle the preview between the before and after versions after you apply a colorization effect.

✦ When you are done with the adjustments, click on Ok

Smoothing Skin

By lessening the sharpness of the skin lines, the Smooth Skin command enables you to swiftly and effectively diminish the appearance of wrinkles in the skin within a face in the Photoshop Element. While doing so contributes to making the skin of the chosen face appear smoother, a slight blurring effect is also applied to the face to achieve this. Remember that this command only functions on faces. Additionally, the command cannot be used with this image if the face is partially hidden.

Follow the procedure below to apply the Smooth Skin command:

- Open the image you want to work on
- Select **Smooth Skin** from the **Enhance menu**

Enhance	Layer	Select	Filter	View	Win
Auto Smart Fix				Alt+Ctrl+M	
Auto Smart Tone...				Alt+Ctrl+T	
Auto Levels				Shift+Ctrl+L	
Auto Contrast			Alt+Shift+Ctrl+L		
Auto Haze Removal				Alt+Ctrl+A	
Auto Color Correction				Shift+Ctrl+B	
Auto Shake Reduction					
Auto Sharpen					
Auto Red Eye Fix				Ctrl+R	
Adjust Color				▸	
Adjust Lighting				▸	
Adjust Smart Fix...				Shift+Ctrl+M	
Convert to Black and White...			Alt+Ctrl+B		
Colorize Photo...				Alt+Ctrl+R	
Haze Removal...				Alt+Ctrl+Z	
Adjust Sharpness...					
Smooth Skin...					
Open Closed Eyes...					
Adjust Facial Features...					
Shake Reduction...					

- In the **Smooth Skin** dialog box, the area to be affected is surrounded by a circle.

- Use the **Smoothness slider** to apply the volume of smoothness you want in the image.

- Use the **Before and After** toggle button to view before and after you apply the **Smooth** effect.

- After the adjustments have been made, you can click on **Ok** to exit and save the changes.

215

Adjusting Facial Features

You can alter a person's lips, eyes, nose, and face in an image in Photoshop Element by using the Adjust Facial Features command. The command won't function with this image if the face is partially hidden.

Follow the instructions listed below to use this command.

✦ Select Adjust Facial Features from the Enhance menu.

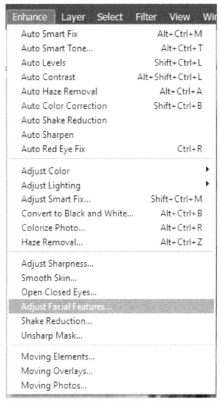

✦ In the **Adjust Facial Features** dialog box, make use of the slider to adjust the facial features such as eyes, nose, lip, chin, and face.

✦ After all the adjustments have been made, click on **Ok**

Reducing Shake

You can manually alter an image using the Wobble Reduction tool to get rid of the blur or shake that happens when holding your camera or phone while shooting a picture. If you don't like the outcomes of the Auto Shake, you can use this option to manually alter the image.

To use the Shake Reduction command, follow the steps below

- ◆ Select the picture you wish to edit

- ◆ Go to the **Enhance menu** and click on **Shake Reduction**

- The **Shake Reduction** dialog box will open and display a selection box over your image.

- Click and drag the resizing handles on the selection box to change to its size.

- Use the **Sensitivity slider** to adjust the amount of sharpening to perform on the image.

- You can use the **Add Another Shake Region** to add another region.

- Use the **Before and After** toggle button to view before and after you apply the **Shake Reduction** effect.

- After all adjustments have been made, click on **Ok**

Moving Photos

Using the Moving Photos command, you can shoot a picture while adding a basic pan, zoom, or rotate effect. You can export the image as an animated gif to turn it into a moving image.

The steps listed below can be used to produce a moving image.

- Open the photo to turn a moving photo in the Photo **Editor**

- Go to the Enhance menu and click on Moving Photos

✦ Here, the **Moving Photos** window is displayed

✦ On the right-hand side, use the **Zoom tool** and the **Hand tool** to zoom and pan the preview image that appears as needed.

✦ Apply the Motion Effects to see the preview of the effect appear on the picture. The Motion Effects appear in the scrollable pane, on the right side of the window.

✦ To toggle **3D Effect** on or off, click the **3D Effect** toggle button at the bottom

✦ Click the play button that appears below the previous image to replay the effect preview after playing an effect.

✦ To export the image as an animated gif, click on **Export** and follow the instructions given.

Moving Elements

This feature is one of the upgrades made to Adobe Photoshop Elements. It is a feature that was not available in the earlier version of the software, This feature permits you to cause motion to elements in a static image.

Follow the procedure below to make moving elements:

- ◆ Open the photo you desire to make modifications to
- ◆ Open the **Enhance menu** and select **Moving Elements**

- Select the area you want to add motion to **with a brush, a quick selection tool, or An Auto selection tool.**
- Click the **Arrow Cursor** and draw your mouse cursor in the direction you desire the motion to go in the area you have selected for modification

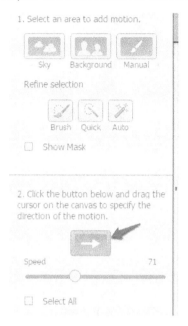

- Determine the speed of the element`s motion by dragging the **speed slider** until you are satisfied with its level of speed.
- Click on the **play button** to see your preview.

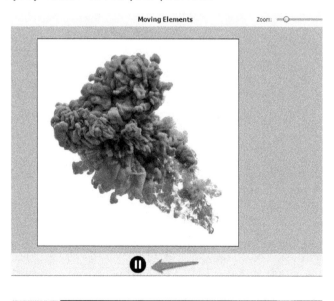

✦ Then click on **Export** to export your file once you are satisfied with your modifications.

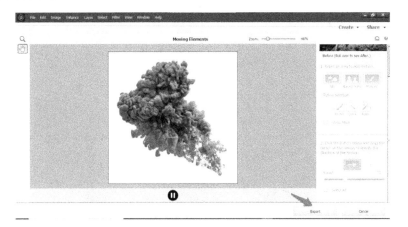

✦ You can either export your file as GIFF or an MP4 Video file.

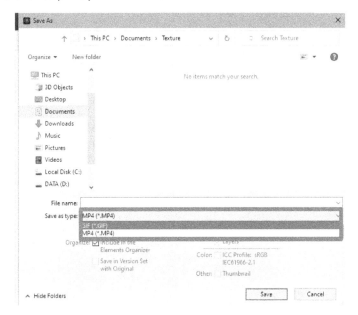

✦ Click on **Save.**

Moving Overlays

The Moving Overlay Command allows you to add overlay animations to your photo. **Overlays, Graphics,** and **Frames** are the three categories of animated elements in the Moving Overlay Command Centre.

To Apply the Moving Overlays to your photo, Follow the procedures below:

✦ Open the photo you desire to edit in the Photo Editor.

✦ Select **Moving Overlays** from the **Enhance** menu.

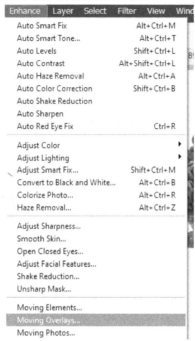

✦ Here, the **Moving Overlays** window is displayed

✦ On the right-hand side, select the kind of **Overlay Animations** you'd love to add to your photo and they are; **Overlays, Graphics,** and **Frames**.

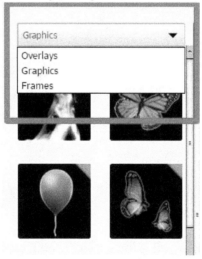

    o   You can protect the subject of your photo from the overlay alteration by clicking on **Protect Subject.**

✦ Use the **Opacity Slider** to adjust the opacity of the added animations.

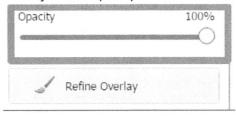

✦ Use the **Refine Overlay** button to move your animation overlay to the desired position.

✦ Click on the **Play button** to see the preview of your modifications.

♦ To export the image as an animated gif, click on Export and follow the instructions given. Then click on **Save**.

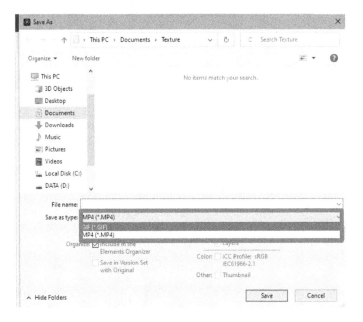

Working Intelligently With The Smart Brush Tools

The last topic we'll cover in this chapter is how to utilize the Smart Brush and Detail Smart Brush tools to add an image modification or a special effect to your photo.

The Smart Brush Tool

By brushing across your image, the Smart Brush tool enables you to utilize a variety of effects selectively. There are 50 preset effects available for selection. This tool has effects for producing and enhancing details, adjusting color and tones, etc. These effects include lipstick, tan, contrast between clouds, infrared, impressionist, various color tints, etc.

Use the instructions listed below to use the Smart Brush tool.

- Go to the **Toolbar** and select the **Smart Brush tool**

- Go to the **Preset menu** to select the effects to apply such as Photographic effects and Nature effects

- Go to the **Brush Settings** drop-down panel to change the bush attributes

- Use the **New, Add, and Subtract Selection** icons to create, add, and subtract selections respectively

- Use the **Refine Edge** to refine the selected area in your image.

- Use the Adjustment layer to fine-tune the adjustment in your image

- When you are done with the adjustments, click on **Ok**

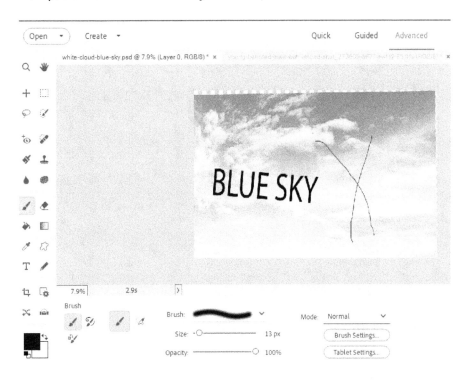

The Detail Smart Brush Tool

Similar to the Smart Brush tool is the Detail Smart Brush tool. The Detail Smart Brush tool is the only difference; it provides you more control over choices and lets you paint adjustments directly into the image.

Use the procedures listed below to use the Detail Smart Brush tool.

- Go to the **Toolbar** and select the **Smart Brush tool**

- Go to the **Preset menu** to select the effects to apply

- Go to the **Brush Settings** drop-down panel to change the bush attributes

- Use the **Refine Edge** to refine the selected area in your image.

- Use the Adjustment layer to fine-tune the adjustment in your image

- When you are done with the adjustments, click on **Ok**

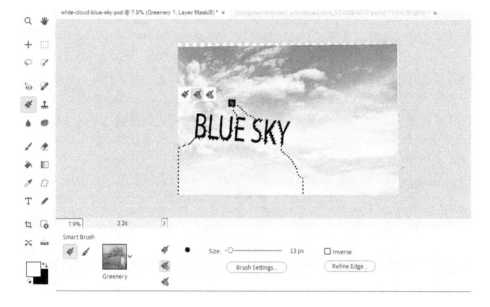

227

CHAPTER THIRTEEN

WORKING WITH TYPES IN PHOTOSHOP ELEMENTS

Using the Photoshop Element, you may easily add text or words to your image in a variety of styles, colors, and effects. To make changes to these texts, you can use the relevant Photoshop Element tools.

Before using the type tool to add text to your image, you must understand the following concept:

- ✦ Tools
- ✦ Modes
- ✦ Formats

Tools

When adding or modifying text to photos, the Photoshop component has seven different tool types. The horizontal and vertical types are the most commonly utilized. The two forms of horizontal type tools. Emphasis will be placed on the two types of horizontal type tools, which are as follows to make these type tools simple to understand:

- ✦ **Type:** This is used to enter type by creating its type layer. Bitman and Index Color are the only modes in the type tool that don't support layering.
- ✦ **Type Mask:** This type of tool only creates a selection border in the shape of the selected type. When the selection boundary is made, the image's active layer is automatically added.

Below are the remaining type tools

- ✦ **Text On Selection:** This tool allows you to create a selection by drawing on your image. Texts applied in the image follow the shape of the path.
- ✦ **Text On Shape:** With this tool, you can draw shapes on your image directly from the shapes menu. Texts applied here also follow the shape.
- ✦ **Text On Custom Path**: With this type of tool, you can draw any custom path you want on your image. Texts inputted.

The Vertical type tools must be used for entering the Chinese and Japanese characters.

Mode

With this method, text is inserted into the picture. Photoshop Elements has three other methods for entering text: path mode, paragraph mode, and point mode.

- ◆ **Point**: This mode is used when you wish to type a few words on your image. Text here can exceed the boundary of your image when entered. To use this mode, go to the Tools Panel, click the n-Type tool, and select the images to start typing.
- ◆ **Paragraph:** To enter more texts on your image in a guarded block, this mode is best suited. With this mode, click and drag the type tool to create a text bounding box to enter your texts. Texts entered do not go beyond the bounding box and in case a line of text is too long, it is wrapped to the next line within the bounding box.
- ◆ **Path:** Here you get to input your texts on a path making use of three unique tools. Double-click on the path and then type the desired texts.

Formats

Here, the Photoshop Element's appearance and print quality are controlled by formats. Depending on your preferences, you choose the format to use. In Photoshop Elements, there are two distinct formats:

- ◆ **Vector:** For texts in the type, this is the default option. This format type provides resizeable ascendable outlines without creating any jagged edges in the diagonal stroke. Additionally, this format type can be altered with a print of higher quality.
- ◆ **Raster:** This is the type of text format that cannot be changed. The texts are automatically rasterized when you convert the vector to pixels. In other words, the text has been replaced with a raster image. When you want to add a filter to your texts or want to include the text alongside the image, the raster format works best. The raster picture either degrades in quality or develops jagged edges every time it is scaled.

How To Create Point Type

As stated earlier, this mode is used when you desire to use a few words on your image which can be headlines, logos, and labels

Follow the procedures below to create a point type.

- ◆ Select the Type Tool from the Toolbar

❖ Select either a **Horizontal** **Type** **Tool** or **Vertical** **Type** **Tool**

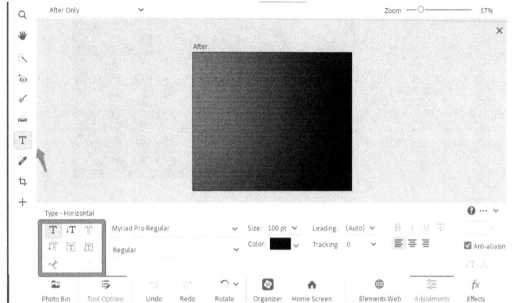

❖ The mouse pointer then transforms into an I-beam directly over the area of the image where you want to enter your text. The baseline on which the text will start or stop is indicated by this character.

❖ Next, click wherever you want the text baseline to appear on the image.

❖ Set the type settings, including font size, font style, font family, etc., from the Tool Options bar.

❖ To build a new text baseline as needed, enter the texts in the text baseline and press the Enter key.

❖ When you are finished typing, press the Commit button to save your changes. Alternatively, you can click the Cancel button to undo your changes.

230

After

Creating a Paragraph Type

As the paragraph is generated, the type's lines will wrap to match the bounding box's dimensions. Using the Tool Options bar, you can enter multiple lines of text and select the proper paragraph alignment. Here, the bounding box's dimensions can be changed to fit the text inside of it. The bounding box is also used to skew, resize, and rotate the texts within it.

Follow the procedures listed below to create the paragraph type.

- Go to the **Toolbar** and select the **Type Tool**
- Choose either a **Horizontal Type Tool** or a **Vertical Type Tool**
- Click and drag the border of the boundary box with your mouse.

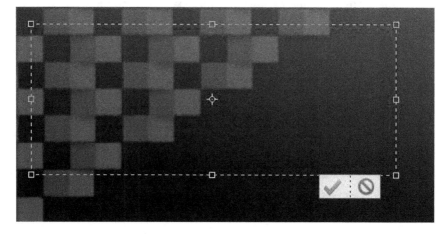

- Set the formatting options from the **Tool Options**

- Type your words into the bounding box
- Click on the **Commit Button** to apply the changes you have made. Alternatively, click on **Cancel Button** to cancel changes.

How To Create Path Type

As was already mentioned, the path type enables you to enter text along a path using three special tools: the Selection tool, the Shape tool, the and Custom path tool. With these tools, you may enter text along a path that flows in a circle, a wave, a stair step, or any other shape you like.

Using The Text On Selection Tool

To use the Text on Selection Tool, follow the steps below

- Go to the **Toolbar,** select the **Selection Tool to make a** selection, **and** then click on **Type Tool**
- In the **Type Tool,** click on **Text On Selection Tool**

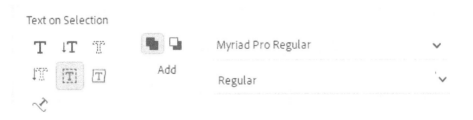

- Click inside the selection made and then click on the **Commit button** where the selection becomes a solid line

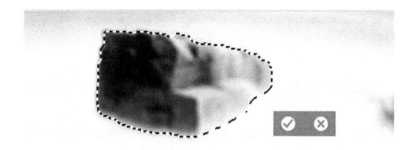

- To add your texts, move the mouse pointer over the line at the location where you want to start adding texts. Here the mouse pointer changes to the I-Beam character, where you begin to add your texts.
- When you are done typing, click on the **Commit button.** Alternatively, you can click on the **Cancel button** to reject all changes.

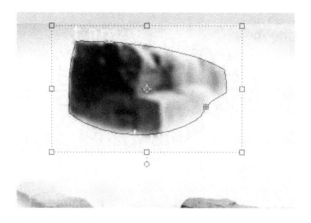

Using The Text On Shape Tool

To use Text on Shape:

- Select the **Shape Tool** from the **Toolbar** to create a shape
- Click on **Text on Shape Tool** in the **Type Tool**

- Select the shape layers in the **Layer Panel**
- To begin inserting your texts, place the mouse pointer over the line at the desired area. When you start adding your text, the mouse cursor turns to the I-Beam character.
- When you're finished, press the **Commit button**. To reject all changes, you can also click the **Cancel option**.

Using The Text On Custom Path Tool

- Select the **Type tool** and select **Text on the Custom Path**.

- At this moment, the mouse pointer changes to a pen icon. Draw the path where you want the text by clicking and dragging. When the mouse is let go, the sketched route solidifies. then select the **Commit Button** to approve the path.

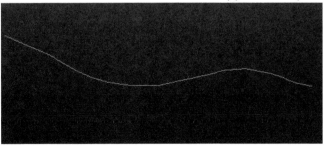

- To begin inserting your texts, place the mouse pointer over the line at the desired area. When you start adding your text, the mouse cursor turns to the I-Beam character.
- When you're finished, press the **Commit button**. To reject all changes, you can also click the **Cancel option**.

Configuring The Type Tool Options

One of the most crucial components of Type is the Type Tool Options box. This is where you get to modify your texts according to your taste and desire. The following are the options found in the Tool Options.

- **Font Family**: This option applies a font family to the new or existing text.
- **Font Style**: This option applies the font styles such as bold, and italics to the new or existing text.
- **Font Size**: This option applies the font size to a new or existing text.
- **Color Menu**: This allows you to add color to the new or selected text from the Color Picker or the Swatches panel.
- **Leading Menu**: This sets the amount of space between the baselines of lines of the new or selected texts.
- **Tracking:** The character spacing of the new or chosen texts is configured using this. The letters are closer together when the space is set to a negative value, whereas gaps between the letters are wider when set to a positive value.
- **Faux Bold:** In addition to getting the bold style from the font style, you may also apply the faux bold to new or existing text to achieve the bold style, however this bold is phony.
- **Faux Italics:** This option helps apply to italics style to the new or existing when the italics style cannot be used in the font style.

- **Underline:** This option helps to apply an underline to the new or selected existing text.
- **Strikethrough:** This option helps to apply a line through the new or selected existing texts.
- **Align Text:** You may control the text orientation thanks to this. If the text is horizontally oriented, you can align it to the left, the center, or the right. If the text is vertically oriented, you can align it to the top, middle, or bottom.
- **Toggle Text Orientation:** This changes the text orientation i.e. vertical to horizontal and vice versa.
- **Wrap Text:** This option enables you to wrap texts on the layers selected
- **Anti-aliased:** This option allows the text on the image to appear smoother or better still, softens the edges of the type.

Editing Your Texts

The Photoshop Element makes text editing much simpler than it appears. You can add, remove, and edit the text in your documents by using the Type Option bar (font size, font styles, font color, etc.)

To delete texts in your image, do the following:

- From the **Toolbox,** select the **Type tool**
- **Double-click** within the text to select the **Text layer**
- Highlight the text by dragging across it with the I-beam of the **Type tool,** and then press the **Backspace Key**
- When you are done, click on the **Commit button.**

To Add Texts

- Select the **Type Tool** from the **Toolbox**
- Double-click within the text to select the **Text Layer**
- Click on the I-beam within the line of the texts and then enter the new texts.
- Click on the **Commit Button** when you are done.

To Change The Font Size, Color, And Other Type Options

- ✦ From the **Toolbox,** select the **Type tool**
- ✦ Double-click within the text to select **the Text layer**
- ✦ Highlight the text by dragging and hovering over it with the I-beam.
- ✦ Go to the **Tool Options** to select the desired changes.
- ✦ After making the desired changes, click on the **Commit button**

Simplifying Type

By "simplifying" (or "rasterizing") your text or type, you imply that you wish to convert it to pixels so that you can add effects like filters, paint, gradients, and patterns. Keep in mind that after your text has been simplified, it cannot be altered once more.

Follow the procedures listed below to simplify the text.

- ✦ Select the layer in the **Layer Panel**
- ✦ Go to the **Menu bar**, select **Layer,** and click on **Layer Simplify** to change the **Vector information** to Bitmap information as shown In the image below.

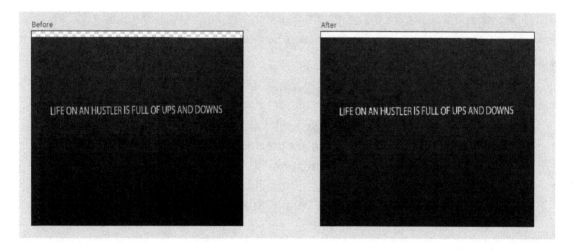

Masking With Type

The Type Mask tool facilitates the creation of selection regions that take the form of written text. The Text Selection can make use of the same fill effects as the Shape Selection. This choice can have a foreground color or a background color applied to it. Making a type mask follows the same steps as making regular text.

The instructions below can be used to construct a type mask.

- ✦ From the **Toolbox,** select the **Type tool**
- ✦ Select either the **Horizontal Type Mask tool** or **Vertical Type Mask tool in the Tool Options bar**

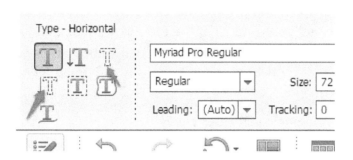

- ✦ Here, a mask is created over the layer, and then create the text either using point or paragraph text styles.

  Set the type option such as font family, style, size, etc. in the **Tool Options.**

- ✦ To apply any fill effects or strokes to the selection created, go to **Edit** and click on **Fill selection** to apply any fill effect you want.

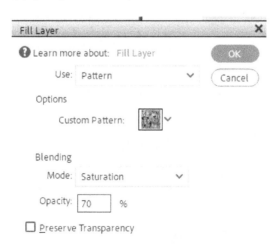

- ✦ Here, the Type Mask is changed to what you want

Warping A Type

You can apply universal shapes to all of the texts by warping the text in the text layer. Applying the arc shape to a text layer, for example, will cause the text to arc like a rainbow. Full strong text cannot be twisted in the same way as bitmap fonts or any other font lacking outline information may.

Do the following to warp text in the text layer:

- Select the Text **Layer** to wrap
- Go to the **Toolbox**, and select the **Type Tool**

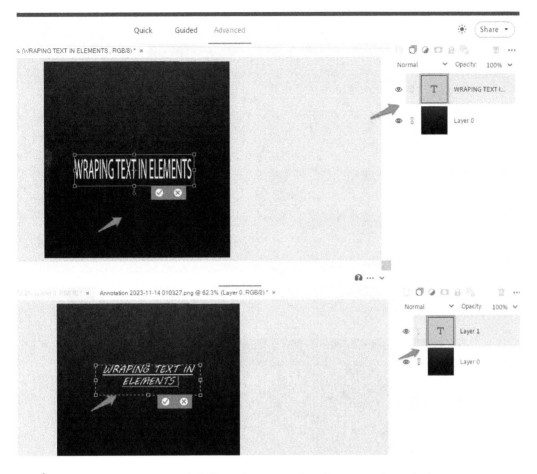

* Go to **Tool Options** and click on the **Warp Text** button to launch the

* Set the options in the **Warp Text** dialog box
    o **Styles:** This displays a drop-down menu where you get to select the shape of the warped text.
    o **Horizontal or vertical**: This allows you to change the orientation of your texts to either Horizontal or Vertical.
    o **Blend**: This is used to set the amount of warp

- o **Horizontal Distortion and Vertical Distortion**: This is used to apply perspective to the warp.

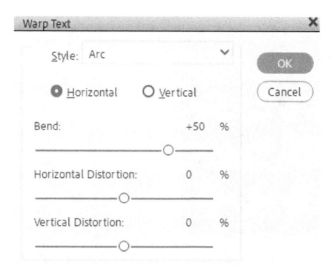

✦ Then click on **Ok**

Unwarping A Type

- ✦ Go to **Type Tool** and select the **Warp** button under the **Tool Options**
- ✦ Select the text layer that has been warped
- ✦ Select **None** under Style in the Warp dialog box.

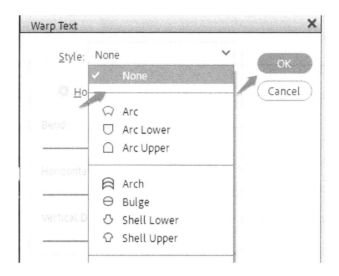

- ✦ Then click on **Ok**

Changing The Orientation Of A Type Layer

- ✦ Select the text and then click the **Toggle Text Orientation** button in the **Tool Options bar.**

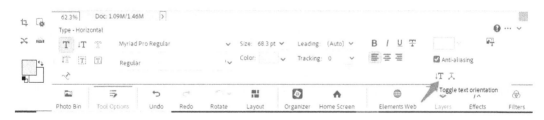

CHAPTER FOURTEEN

CREATING PHOTO PROJECTS

This chapter of this book takes you on a journey of how to go creative with your images. With your photos, you can create a photo book, greeting cards, collages, and other kinds of projects with your photographs.

With Photoshop Element you can create these projects and share them online, print them using a computer printer, and even save them on your hard drive.

To start this project, open the **Organizer** on your Photoshop Element and select **Create** to start a photo project. On the drop-down menu, you have the list of the options available for creating photo projects.

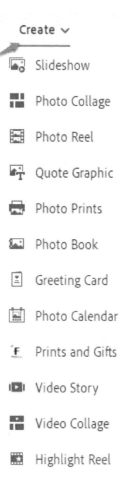

Creating Slideshows

Making slideshows with Photoshop Elements is a fantastic way to showcase your photos with others. Add text, captivating transitions, and audio recordings to make an amazing presentation.

Photoshop Elements lets you create slideshows from the photos you've selected from The Organizer. With Photoshop Elements, you can also use the open photos in the "Photo Bin" of the Photo Editor to create slideshows. But remember that images with unsaved edits cannot be used in the Photo Editor unless you save the changes beforehand.

You can either create your slideshows directly from the **Organizer** or through the **Photo Editor.** However, using the **Photo Editor** will still direct you to the **organizer**.

Follow the procedure below to be able to create a slideshow:

- ✦ Open the pictures to be used in Photoshop Element right in the **Photo Editor** or **Organizer**. The pictures opened will be displayed in the Photo Bin. However, keep in mind that you cannot use photos in the Photo Editor that contain unsaved changes unless you save the changes beforehand.
- ✦ Click on **Create** and **Slideshow** in the drop-down menu

- ✦ Clicking on **Slideshow** will open up the **Organizer** and your slideshow begins to play at once.
- ✦ Toolbars can be shown above, below, and to the left of the slideshow as it is being played. These three toolbars contain buttons that can be used to edit, save, export, or stop a slideshow as well as control how it plays back

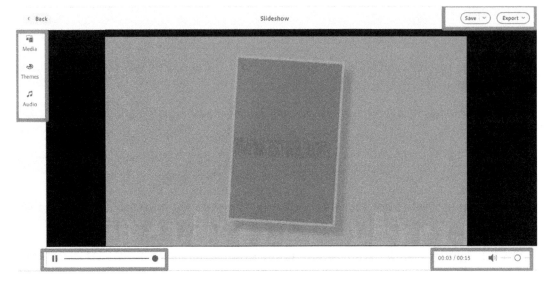

✦ You may regulate the slideshow's playback and volume using the bottom toolbar's playback scrubber and volume setting.

✦ To fast-forward or rewind the slideshow, click and drag the little dot in the timeline scrubber.

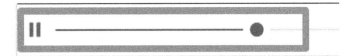

✦ The playback can be paused by clicking the "Pause" button at the left end of the toolbar. This button becomes the "Play" button when you click it, and you can click it again to restart playback.

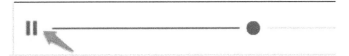

✦ The toolbar at the left-hand side of the slideshow consists of **Media, Themes,** and **Audio buttons. The Media** button allows you to add captions to your images. **Theme** allows you to modify your slideshow's display while the **Audio** button allows you to add music to the slideshow.

* On the toolbar at the top of the window, select **Save**.

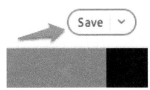

* When you do this, the "Elements Organizer" dialog box appears. To save the slideshow, type a name for it and then click "**Save**." The "**Save**" button only saves any modifications that haven't been saved after a slideshow has been saved.

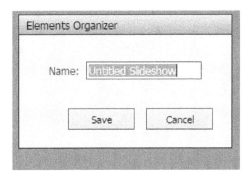

* Click the drop-down button at the right side of the "Save" button. Then choose the "Save As" command from the pop-up menu that appears.

- Click on the **Export** to export the slideshow choose one of the options from the drop-down menu that appears: "YouTube," "Vimeo," or "Export video to local disk.

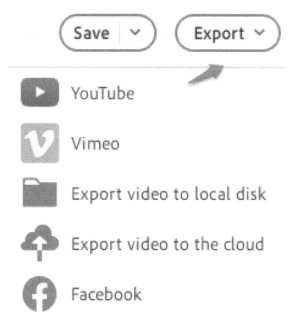

- If you choose the **Export video to local disk** command. In the **Filename** area, provide a name for the slideshow video. The **Location** column displays the default folder to save the file into. Clicking the **Browse** button will bring up a **Browse for Folder** window where you can choose a different place. After that, pick a new destination folder and press **OK**.
- To choose the HD quality of the video to be produced, use the drop-down in the **Quality** section. The slideshow will then be exported as a video file when you click the **OK** button.

Export

Filename

Location

C:\Users\A ▦ ▦Videos\

(Browse)

Quality

Preset: 720p HD   ⌄

(OK) (Cancel)

Creating Photo Collages

A photo collage is made up of many images that have been pieced together artistically. As a result, making a photo collage enables you to display multiple images simultaneously.

Follow these steps to make a photo collage.

- ⬍ Right in the **Photo Editor or Organizer**, open the images that will be utilized in Photoshop Element. The opened photos will be shown below in the Photo Bin.
- ⬍ Select **Photo Collage** from the drop-down menu by clicking **Create**.

Create ⌄

🖼 Slideshow

▦ Photo Collage

▦ Photo Reel

🖼 Quote Graphic

🖨 Photo Prints

🖼 Photo Book

▣ Greeting Card

🖼 Photo Calendar

❖ When this is done loading, The photo collage is displayed in a random layout like the image below.

❖ There are four types of layouts in the photo collage; **Horizontal**, **Vertical**, **Panorama,** and **Square**. You can pick your choice of layout from the upper right-hand of the Menu.

- ✦ You can add a photo or any image in the photo collage, by either dragging the image of choice from the Photo Bin, picking from your computer, or, the Organizer.
  - o **Dragging from the Photo Bin:**

  - o **Adding from Your Computer:**

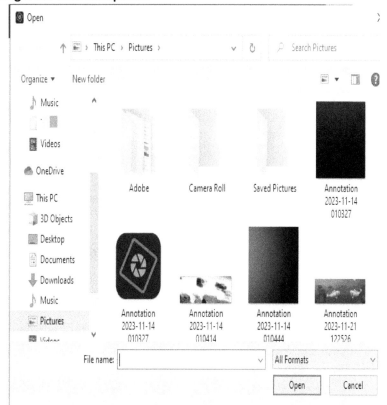

  - o **Adding from the organizer:**

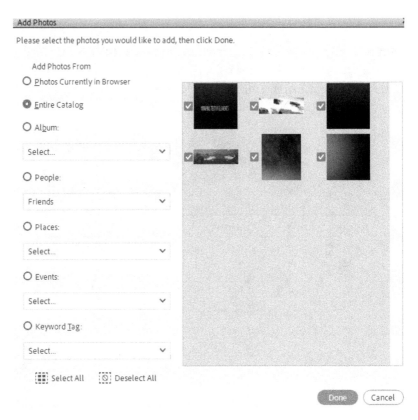

- Use the **Slider bar** to zoom in or out on the collage

- Select **Pages** to add or delete pages

- Select **Graphics** to choose a background or a frame and double-click on the background or frame to apply to the collage.

- You can set your collage to either **Advanced Mode** or **Basic Mode**

  - **Advanced Mode:** With this mode, you get to use the complete toolbox and layer options, which can be used to retouch images and edit layers.

  - **Basic Mode:** This allows you to add and move texts and graphics.

- Click on **Save** to save your photo collage in the different formats you want.

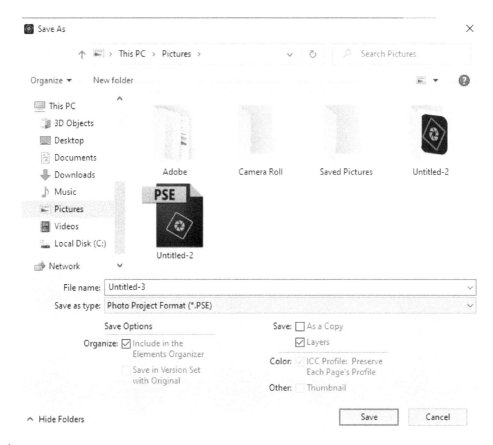

♦ To print your photo collage, click on **Print**.

Create Quote Graphic

The Quote Graphic feature was first introduced into the Photoshop Adobe Photoshop Elements 2021 and it deviates from the way we create Photo Collages, Photo Books, and Greeting Cards.

Follow the Procedure below to create a Quote Graphic

♦ Open the pictures to be used in Photoshop Element right in the **Photo Editor** or **Organizer**. The pictures opened will be displayed down in the Photo Bin.

♦ Click on **Create** and select **Quote Graphic** in the drop-down menu

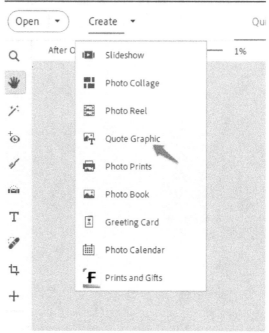

- The first window appears and displays the available templates for your selection.

- The **Start From The Scratch** icon allows you to start over without utilizing a template, as demonstrated below while the **Start With A Photo** allows you to pick an image for your template.

- Select the template you want to use. The panel immediately changes to an assortment of fixed sizes and sharing destinations. For example, you can make an Instagram post, a Facebook Cover, a Twitter, or a Pinterest post. You can select from a variety of fixed sizes that you can open in the Photo Editor, as shown if you don't wish to post to a social media website.

- The **Background/Effects panel** appears when you select a choice in the Template size panel.

254

- The **Backdrop panel** is the default, and from there you can pick from a variety of background patterns and colors. You can select from a wide range of various effects by clicking the **Effects panel**.

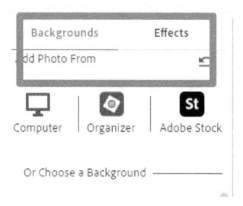

- Below the Background/Effect panel are four more tools: **Background**, **Text**, **Style**, and **Animate.**
  - o **Background** allows you to change the background of your photo
  - o **Text** allows you to edit/add text to your image.
  - o **Style** permits you to modify the layout of your image and texts
  - o **Animate** gives motion to your work.

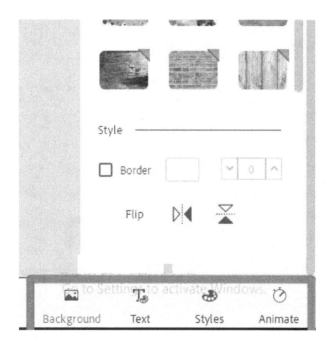

- Open the **Photo Bin** in the Photo Editor and drag a new photo to the document to replace the existing one.
- Click the **Save** button that appears at the bottom of the Background/Effects panels to save your work when you are done.

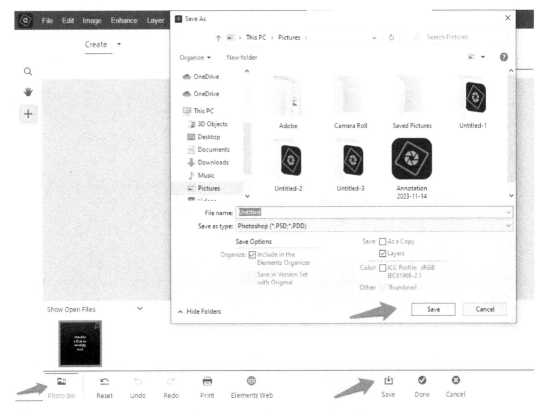

- Export your work by using the **Save As** feature in the **File** menu.

Creating Photo Print

This allows you to print your image via a **local printer**, **Picture package, and contact Sheet.**

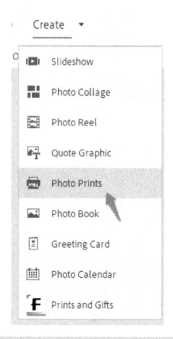

Creating Photo Books

A photo book is a book that uses photographs to convey its content, whether there are writings present or not. The photo book is a terrific way to save your and your loved ones' memories.

- ✦ Use these steps to make a photo book. Open the pictures to be used in Photoshop Element right in the **Photo Editor** or **Organizer**

- ✦ Go to **Create** and click on **Photo Book**

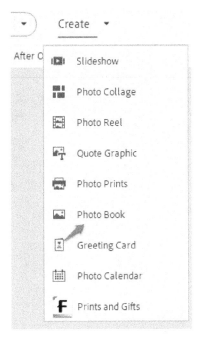

Create ▾

After O

Slideshow

Photo Collage

Photo Reel

Quote Graphic

Photo Prints

Photo Book

Greeting Card

Photo Calendar

F Prints and Gifts

◆ Select the following options in the Photo Book dialog box, then click "Ok."

`Select the size of the photo book

o Select the theme to apply to the photobook

o Click on the **Autofill with Selected Images** checkmark to use the images you selected in the Photo Bin

o Set the number of pages in the photo book ranging from 2 to 78

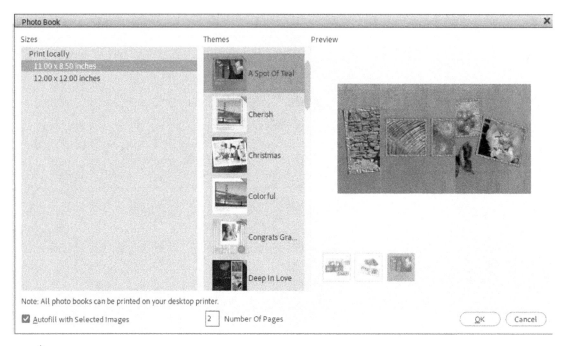

✤ When the project is opened, the options listed below are visible in the lower-right corner:

    o **Pages:** To display the pages of the photo book.

    o **Layout:** To display the current layout of the photo book. With this option, you can change the layout of your photo book.

    o **Graphics:** With this option, you can change the background, frame, and graphics in the photo book.

✤ You can set your collage to either **Advanced Mode** or **Basic Mode** (These modes are used interchangeably and are located underneath the Create option)

    o **Advanced Mode:** With this mode, you get to use the complete toolbox and layer options, which can be used to retouch images and edit layers.

o **Basic Mode:** This allows you to add and move texts and graphics

✦ Click on **Save** to save your photo book in the different formats you want.

✦ To print your photo book, click on **Print.**

Creating Greeting Cards

An illustrated message on a greeting card can be used to convey feelings of love, friendship, gratitude, sympathy, or other emotions. Use the following instructions to make a greeting card.

✦ Right in the **Photo Editor or Organizer** for the greeting card, open the images that will be used in Photoshop Element.

✦ Select **Greeting Cards** under **Create**.

✦ Set the following parameters in the Greeting Card dialog box, then click "Ok."
   o Decide on the greeting card's size.
   o Decide on a theme for the greeting card.
   o To use the photos you chose in the Photo Bin, click the **Autofill with Selected Images** checkbox.

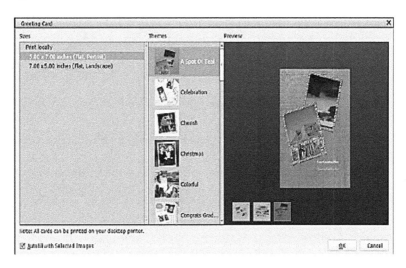

- After the project has been opened, the following options are displayed in the lower-right corner:

  - **Pages:** To display the pages of the greeting card

  - **Layout:** To display the current layout of the greeting card. With this option, you can change the layout of your greeting card.

  - **Graphics:** With this option, you can change the background, frame, and graphics in the greeting card.

- You can set your greeting card to either **Advanced Mode** or **Basic Mode**

  - **Advanced Mode:** With this mode, you get to use the complete toolbox and layer options, which can be used to retouch images and edit layers.

  - **Basic Mode:** This allows you to add and move texts and graphics

- Click on **Save** to save your greeting card in the different formats you want.

- To print your greeting card, click on **Print.**

- Click on **Save** to save your greeting card in the different formats you want.

- To print your greeting card, click on **Print.**

Creating Photo Calendars

The photo calendars help to share your loved moments creatively. To create a photo calendar, follow the steps below

- Choose the pictures you like to showcase in the Photo Editor or Organizer for your photo calendar.

- Go to **Create** and select **Photo Calendar**

- In the **Photo Calendar** dialog box, set the following options and click on **Ok.**

  - Select the starting month and year of the photo calendar.

  - Select the size of the photo calendar.

  - Select the theme to apply to the photo calendar

261

o Click on the **Autofill with Selected Images** checkmark to use the images you selected in the Photo Bin

* After the project has been opened, the following options are displayed in the lower-right corner:

   o **Pages:** To display the pages of the photo card

   o **Layout:** To display the current layout of the photo card. With this option, you can change the layout of your greeting card.

   o **Graphics:** With this option, you can change the background, frames, and graphics in the photo calendar

* You can set your photo calendar to either **Advanced Mode** or **Basic Mode**

   o **Advanced Mode:** With this mode, you get to use the complete toolbox and layer options, which can be used to retouch images and edit layers.

   o **Basic Mode:** This allows you to add and move texts and graphics

* Click on **Save** to save your photo calendar in the different formats you want.

* To print your photo calendar, click on **Print.**

CHAPTER FIFTEEN

GETTING FAMILIAR WITH FILTERS, PHOTO MERGE, STYLES, BLEND MODES, AND LOTS MORE

Working With Filters

One of Photoshop Element's most important and intriguing features are the Filters. In Photoshop Elements, Filters are used for image cleaning and retouching. You may add unique effects or make incredible photo adjustments by leveraging the distortion effects of filters. Some filters are available through plug-ins created by third parties and installed in the Adobe Photoshop Element.

There are three different ways to apply filters in Photoshop Element, and they are as follows.

❖ **Filter Menu**: You may apply each filter individually, and the Filter menu has all the filters you require. Go to the Menu bar to find the File menu.

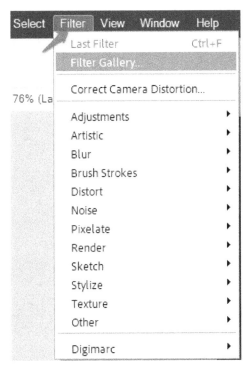

❖ **Filter Gallery**: The Filter Galley shows thumbnails of the filters. You can reorder the filters and modify the parameters in the filter gallery to achieve your goals. However, not all of the filters seen in the Filter menu are present in the Filter

Gallery. Go to **Filter**, choose **Filter Gallery**, choose a category, and then click on the layer you want to apply the filter on.

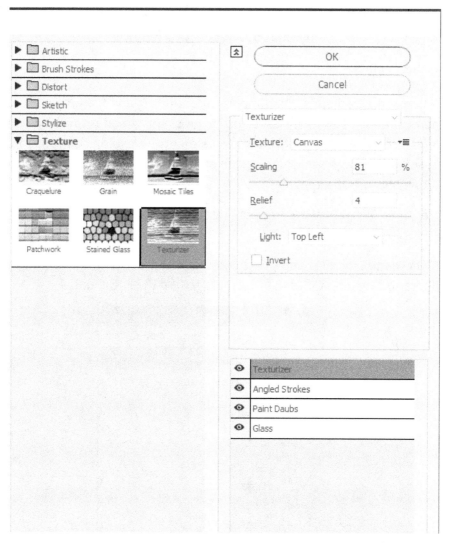

◆ **Filter Panel:** All of the filters that are offered in the Filter menu are displayed as thumbnails in the Filter panel. This is only applicable in Advanced mode. Go to the workspace's lower right corner and select **Filter** to use in this mode.

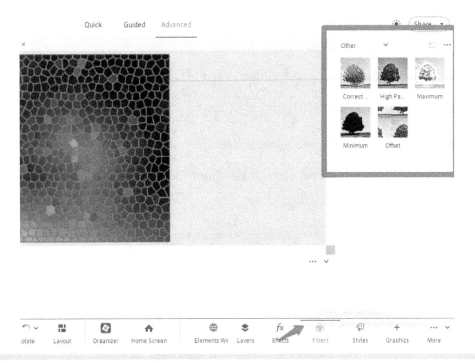

Hints To Observe While Applying Filters

- ✦ Even though the advice seems straightforward, it greatly broadens your perspective on how filters are used.
- ✦ View the filter's result before applying it: Viewing the filter's result before applying it yields the same outcome. Utilizing the preview can save you time.
- ✦ Filters can only be used on an image's active area.
- ✦ Not all photographs can be affected by filters. Pictures in grayscale format, bitmap or indexed-color mode, or 16-bit images are a few examples of these.
- ✦ The mere fact that a filter has already been applied to a picture does not preclude its subsequent application to the same image.

Hints For Creating Visual Effects With Filters

The following guidelines can be used to use filters to achieve unique visual effects.

- ✦ Feathering the selection will smooth out the edges of the filter's effects before applying it to a selection.
- ✦ You can apply filters gradually to ensure a striking result. Additionally, you can use several mixing modes to combine the results of the filters you've used.

♦ You can add filters to photographs that are in solid colors or grayscale to make textures and backdrops.

Applying filters will improve the uniformity and quality

Applying Filter Features

Here, we'll use the Filter Gallery to apply the filter.

The instructions below explain how to use the Filter Gallery to apply a filter to an image.

♦ Select Filter Gallery under Filter

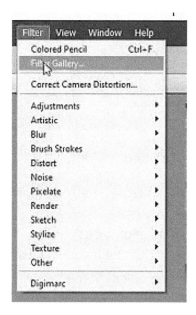

♦ To display specific filter effects inside a category, select the name of the category that is displayed as a folder in the main pane. then choose the filter of your choice.

✦ Set the settings related to the filter as shown in the image below

✦ In the editing window, click the New Effect Layer option to add a new filter.
✦ Select the Delete Effect Layer button to remove a filter.
✦ Once you're finished, select Ok to apply the filters and then click the editing window to close.

The Filter Categories

You must comprehend the many types of filters before applying them to your photographs. These categories are as follows.

- ✢ **Correct Camera Distortion**: This filter aids in the correction of vignetting, barrel and pincushion distortion, and other typical lens faults. Additionally, this filter can fix vertical or horizontal camera tilt-related image perspective issues.
- ✢ **Adjustment filters**: These filters are used to alter an image's pixels' brightness, color, grayscale, and tonal levels. The color pixels in this filter can also be converted to black and white.
- ✢ **Artistic filters**: These are applied to conventional media to improve the painterly appearance and produce a distinctive look.
- ✢ **Blur Filters**: These filters soften an image or a selection.
- ✢ **Brush Stroke** Filters: This filter creates a painterly or fine-art appearance with several brush and ink stroke effects.
- ✢ **Distort filters**: These reshape the image and distort it mathematically to produce 3D effects.
- ✢ **Noise Filters**: This is used to remove dust and scratches from images and also blend a selection of images into the surrounding pixels.
- ✢ **Pixelate filters**: These are used to stamp pixels with similar color values to define an image or selection.
- ✢ The **Render Filter** is what gives an image effect like fibers, lens flare, and lightning.
- ✢ **Sketch Filters**: This gives a hand-drawn appearance by adding texture.
- ✢ **Stylize Filter**: By moving pixels and boosting contrast, this filter creates an impressionistic or painted look.
- ✢ **Texture filters**: These filters aid in giving an image a sense of depth, substance, or an organic appearance.
- ✢ **Other Filters**: With a filter, you may modify the mask, rebalance a selection in an image, and quickly tweak colors. You can also design your filter effects.
- ✢ The Digimarc watermark is read using the **Digimarc filter**.

Using The Liquify Filter

You can wreak havoc on an image, layer, or selection using the Liquify Filter. You may now twist, pinch, pull, and inflate a portion of an image or selection with this technique.

To use the Liquify Filter, follow the steps below

269

- Choose the image you wish to apply the effect to
- Go to **Filter,** select **Distort,** and click on **Liquify.**

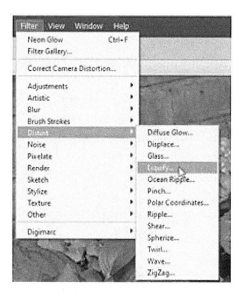

- At the right-hand side of the **Liquify** dialog box, set the following options

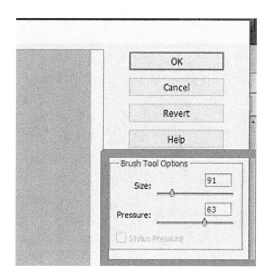

- At the left-hand side of the **Liquify** dialog box, you get to choose the following brushes of your choice

  o **Whirl (W):** This tool pushes the pixel forward as you drag, thus causing a stretching effect.

- **Twirl Clockwise (R) and Twirl Counterclockwise (L):** The Twirl Clockwise spins the pixel you click and drag over in a clockwise direction while the Twirl Counterclockwise spins the pixels in the opposite direction.
- **The Pucker Tool (P):** This tool pulls the sides of the brushstroke inward towards the center of the brushstroke.
- **The Bloat Tool (B):** This pushes the pixels from the center of a brush towards the outer edge of the brush.
- **The Shift Pixel Tool (S):** This tool moves pixels in a perpendicular direction from the direction in which you drag the brushstroke.
- **The Reconstruct Tool (R):** This tool reconstructs the area of the image that you that has been distorted.
- **The Zoom Tool:** This is used to zoom in and out on the image to get a better view of the distortions.
- **Hand Tool (H):** This tool allows you to move around the image in the preview window.

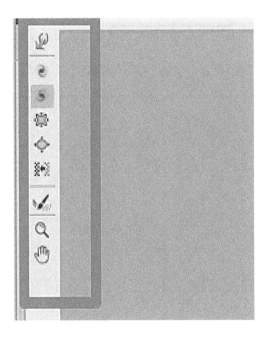

- ✦ Click on the **Revert button** at the right-hand side of the **Liquify** dialog box to reverse all changes made in the current session.
- ✦ Click on **Ok** to apply the distortions and then close the dialog box.

  - **Brush Size:** Here, drag the slider to set the width of the brush or enter a value ranging from 1 to 15,00 pixels to set the width of the brush.
  - **Brush Pressure:** Drag the slider to set or adjust the pressure or enter a value ranging from 1 to 100.

o **Stylus Pressure**: This is used to set the pressure of the stylus.

Correcting Camera Distortion

This is one of the image-filtering techniques you can employ to correct a variety of distortions that arise when shooting pictures. For instance, snapping a photo of a tall skyscraper from the ground can alter your perception of the structure.

Follow the instructions below to utilize the Camera Distortion.

✦ Select **Camera Distortion** from the **Filter** Menu

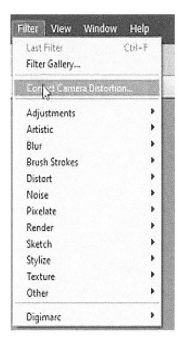

✦ Click on **Preview** to see the original or distorted image in the **Camera Distortion** dialog box.
✦ In the Camera Distortion, set the following correction options.

o **Remove Distortion:** This corrects the lens barrel which is the bloacenterntre of an image caused by wide-angle lenses and pincushions for images that appear pinched in centimeters which can be caused by zoom lenses,
o **Vignette Amount:** This is used to adjust lighting or darkening around the edges of photos caused by poor lenses.
o **Vertical Perspective:** This corrects distorted vertical perspectives from a tilted camera.

o **Horizontal Perspective:** This corrects distorted horizontal perspectives from a tilted camera.

o **Angle**: This corrects distortion caused by tilting the camera. With this option, you can rotate the image.

o **Edge Extension Scale**: This fits your image to scale after correcting your perspective.

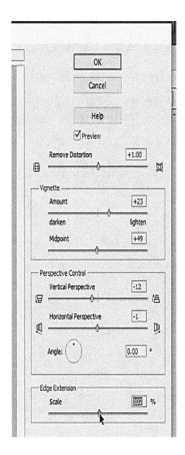

✧ Click on the **Ok** button after making your changes.

Working With Photomerge

This collection of guided edits makes it simple to perform complex photo manipulation. By taking two or more photographs and combining them into one, you may make gorgeous composites using the Photomerge capabilities. In this lesson, we'll learn how to utilize the Photomerge command to combine photographs, which is its primary purpose.

Remember that the Guided Edit mode is the only one where the Photomerge features can be utilized.

PHOTOMERGE COMPOSE

Extract an object from one photo and add it to another.

PHOTOMERGE EXPOSURE

Blend shots with different exposures to get perfect lighting every time.

PHOTOMERGE FACES

Have fun by blending faces from two different photos into one.

Photomerge Panorama

Follow the instructions below to use the Photomerge Panorama.

PHOTOMERGE PANORAMA

Create a panoramic photo by stitching together multiple photos.

- Select the images you wish to use
- In the **Guided Edit mode**, select the **Photomerge** tab and click on **Panorama**
- In the **Panorama Settings**, select any of the following
  - **Auto Panorama:** This option analyses the image source image and either applies a Perspective or Cylindrical layout.
  - **Perspective**: This produces a steady composition by making one of the source images a reference image.
  - **Cylindrical:** This helps to reduce the bow-tie distortion that can happen using the Perspective layout to show an individual image as an unfolded cylinder.

- Spherical: This helps to align and change images as if they were mapping inside a sphere.
- Collage: This aligns the layers and matches overlapping content and changes them to any of the source layers.
- Reposition: This also aligns layers and matches overlapping content but does not change them to any source image.
- Use the settings below to modify the appearance of the Panorama
  - Blend Image Together: This is used to fix the color interval that can take place from matching images with different exposures.
  - Vignette Removal: This is used to fix exposure issues caused by lens flaws.
  - Geometric Distortion Correction: This corrects distortions such as barrel, pincushion, or fisheye distortion.
  - Content-Aware Fill Transparent Areas: This flawlessly fills the transparent area with similar image content.

- When you are done with the changes, click on Create Panorama
- Finally, you can save the image or continue the editing.

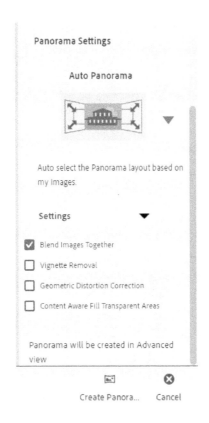

Photomerge Group Shot

You may combine several photographs into one perfect group shot using the Photomerge Group Shot tool.

PHOTOMERGE GROUP SHOT
Make sure everyone in your group shot is smiling and has their eyes open by blending multiple shots into one.

Here are the procedures to create a Photomerge Group Slot.

- Select the images you wish to use
- In the **Guided Edit mode**, select the **Photomerg**e tab and click on **Photomerge Group Shot**
- **From the Photo Bin, select the best pictures and drag them to the Final window**
- To mark the area you want to merge, fine-tune, and add contents to in your image, **use the Pencil tool**
- **To remove content, use the Eraser tool.**
- **Set the following options**
  - o **Show Strokes:** This option displays the Pencil stroke marked in the source image.
  - o **Show Regions:** This shows the regions selected in the final image.
  - o **Advanced Options:** This collapse and expand the arrow for Advanced Options
  - o **Adjustment Tool:** This option helps to fix the alignment of multiple photos.
  - o **Pixel Blending:** This is used to blend or match pixels.

- After making the changes, click on **Next** to either **Save, Continue Editing,** or **Share**.

Photomerge Scene Cleaner

PHOTOMERGE SCENE CLEANER

Easily remove moving objects, like cars, from a series of photos.

The Photomerge Scene Cleaner command enables you to combine many photographs into a single, faultless photo scene by removing extraneous objects, such as cars and onlookers, from the scene.

Follow the instructions below to utilize the Photomerge Scene Cleaner.

- ⬍ Select the images you wish to use
- ⬍ In the **Guided Edit mode**, select the **Photomerge** tab and click on **Photomerge Group Shot Scene Cleaner**
- ⬍ **From the Photo Bin, select the best pictures and drag them to the Final window**

277

- ✦ To mark the area you want to merge, fine-tune, and add contents to in your image, **use the Pencil tool**
- ✦ To remove content, **use the Eraser tool.**
- ✦ **Set the following options**
  - ○ **Show Strokes:** This option displays the Pencil stroke marked in the source image.
  - ○ **Show Regions:** This shows the regions selected in the final image.
  - ○ **Advanced Options:** This collapse and expand the arrow for Advanced Options
  - ○ **Adjustment Tool:** This option helps to fix the alignment of multiple photos.
  - ○ **Pixel Blending:** This is used to blend or match pixels.

- ✦ After making the changes, click on **Next** to either **Save, Continue Editing,** or **Share.**

Photomerge Exposure

PHOTOMERGE EXPOSURE
Blend shots with different exposures to get
perfect lighting every time.

You can disclose an image that has an exposure problem by using the background and foreground using the **Photomerge Exposure command**. For instance, the foreground image has a torch, but the background image is dark. Combining the two photographs will make the image's exposure difficult.

However, there are two ways to use Photomerge Exposure: **Automatic and Manual Photomerge Exposure**

Manuel Photomerge Exposure

- ⬍ Select two or more images to use
- ⬍ In the **Guided Edit mode**, select the **Photomerge** tab and click on **Photomerge Exposure.**
- ⬍ In the **Photomerge Exposure** option, select **Manual mode.**
- ⬍ **In case you choose the Manual mode, do the following**
- ⬍ From the **Photo Bin,** select the pictures (the source image and the final image) and drag them to the **Final window.**
- ⬍ **To draw over the well-exposed area you wish to keep or maintain, use the Pencil tool.**
- ⬍ **To deselect any region selected by the Pencil tool, use the Eraser tool.**
- ⬍ **Set the following**
  - ○ **Show Strokes:** This option displays the Pencil stroke marked in the source image.
  - ○ **Show Regions:** This shows the regions selected in the final image.

- o **Opacity Slider:** This is used to change the transparency of the selected regions to blend them properly in the background.
- o **Edge Blending:** This is used to smoothen the blended edges

✦ After making the changes, click on **Next** to either **Save, Continue Editing,** or **Share.**

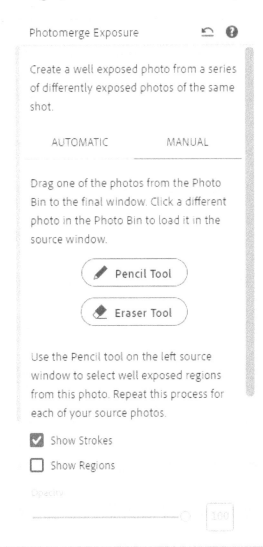

Automatic Photomerge Exposure

To use the Automatic Photomerge Exposure, follow the steps given below

✦ Select two or more images to use

- In the **Guided Edit mode**, select the **Photomerg**e tab and click on **Photomerge Exposure.**
- In the **Photomerge Exposure** option, select **Automatic mode.**
- **Select any of the following options**
  - o **Simple Blending:** This option does not allow for adjusting the Photomerge Exposure settings, rather it displays the merged image.
  - o **Smart Blending:** This option allows for adjusting the Photomerge Exposure settings such as Highlight, Shadows, and Saturation, before merging the image.

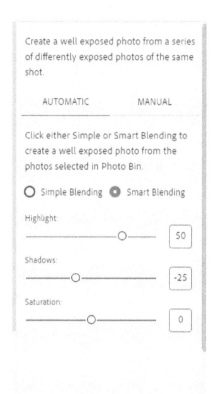

- After making the changes, click on **Next** to either **Save, Continue Editing,** or **Share.**

281

Photomerge Compose

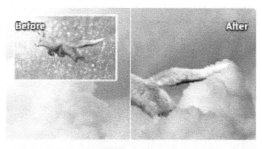

PHOTOMERGE COMPOSE

Extract an object from one photo and add it to another.

You can transfer content from one image to another with the Photomerge Compose command.

Follow these procedures to use this command.

- Select two or images to use
- In the **Guided Edit mode**, select the **Photomerge** tab and click on **Photomerge Composure**
- Drag the image you wish to extract an element from the Photo Bin into the photo editing area.
- Select any of the Selection tools
  - ○ **Quick Select:** This is used to brush over your image to select the element you want
  - ○ **Outline Select:** This is used to trace around the element you want in your image.

- To refine your selection, use the **Refine Selection Brush tool.**
- To set the background**, click on Advance Edge refinement.**
- Click on **Next** and the extracted image is displayed on the second image, making it the new background**.**
- Move and resize the extracted image by dragging it within the bounding box**.**
- Use the **Auto Match Color Tone** to blend the color of the extracted image with the new background.

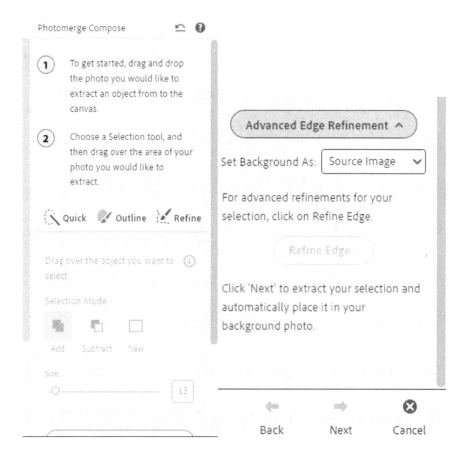

* After making the changes, click on **Next** to either **Save**, **Continue Editing** or **Share**

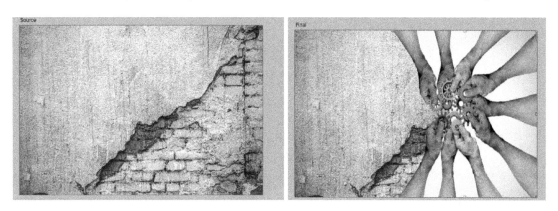

Working With Photo Effect

You may apply picture effects from a single location using the Effects panel. The Effects panel is typically seen in Quick and Expert mode on the taskbar. The artwork or effects that you can add to or apply to an image are shown as thumbnail examples. A menu of category options and related subcategories is available for the majority of sections. You have a choice between three effect categories: **Artistic, Classic,** and **Color Match**.

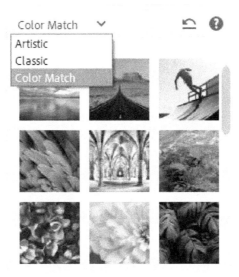

In the **Artistic Effect** section, transform your images in a single click by applying effects that are based on well-known artwork or current artistic trends. Choose from a variety of stunning artistic effects to apply to all or a portion of your shot, and then simply tweak the outcomes to achieve the desired appearance. In Quick and Expert settings, creative effects are available.

Follow these steps to add an artistic impact to your photo:

- ✦ To add a photo in either Quick mode or Expert mode, click **Open**.
- ✦ To choose from 30 artistic effects, click **Effects** and choose **Artistic** on the right panel.
- ✦ To add any **artistic effect** of your choice to your photo, simply click on it.
- ✦ Do the following:
    - o Define **Intensity**
    - o By selecting **Keep original photo colors**, the photo's original colors will be preserved.
    - o You can decide to take the creative effect out of the photo's topic and/or background.
    - o Click **Expert** to recompose the image or specific portions of the image. To mask the areas of the photo you want to recompose, utilize the **Brush in Tool Options.** You can specify **Size** and **Threshold** as well.

Artistic ⌄ ↰ ❷

♦ To save the image, go to **File > Save As**, or to post it on social media, go to **Share**.

In the **Classic Effect** Section, You may add several effects to your phosphating the Photo Effects. The Effect panel has effects including Faded Photos, Glow, Monotone Color, Texture, Panel, and Vintage.

Apply the following to your image to add an effect:

- Select the image you wish to apply the effect to
- Go to **Window** and click on **Eff**ect. Alternatively, You can also select **Effect** by clicking on the **Effect icon** in the bottom right of the workspace.

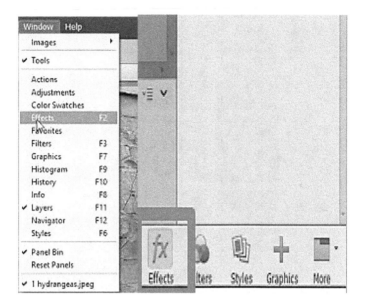

- The Effect panel is displayed on the right-hand side of the workspace, where you select the categories of effect to apply

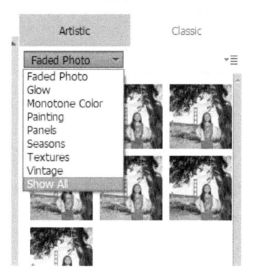

- Select any effect and then apply it to the image
- To save the image, go to **File** > **Save As**, or to post it on social media, go to **Share**.

There are numerous options available in the **Color Match** category, any option selected colorizes the hue of your image with the chosen color.

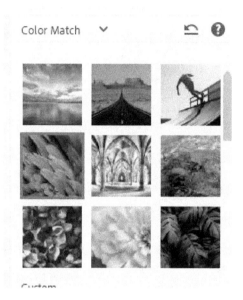

You can use the **Hue**, **Saturation,** and **Brightness Slider** to determine how each color option blends with your image.

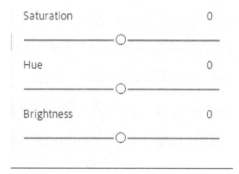

Applying Layers Styles

You can add several effects to the content of a layer using the Layer Styles, like light, shadows, embossed edges, neon, plastic, etc. The layer Style cannot be applied to a specific object or element within a layer; it can only be applied to the entire layer.

Follow these steps to apply the Styles.

- Select the image or layer you wish to apply to the styles

✦ Go to **Window** and select **Styles**. Alternatively, you can use the styles by clicking on **Styles** in the bottom right-right corner of the workspace.

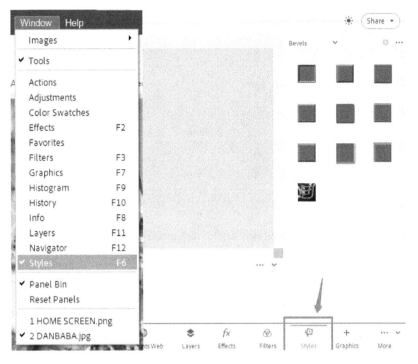

✦ Select the categories of style from the drop-drop at the top of the panel.

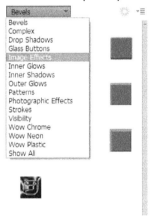

✦ Select the style you want from the **Style Panel**

✦ Go to **Layer**, select **Layer Style**, and then choose any of the options in the drop-down list that suit your need To edit a style`s setting, scale, hide, or show, copy and paste a layer style.

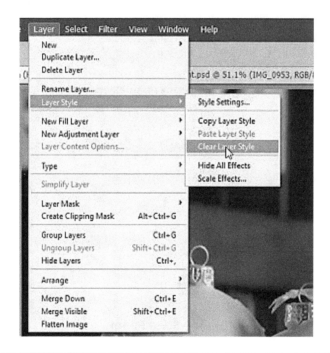

Working With Graphics Panel

You can embellish your image with exciting artwork, theme decorations, frames, shapes, and text styles with the Graphics panel's tool.

Follow these steps to utilize the Graphics panel:

- Select the image or layer you wish to apply to the styles to
- Go to **Windows** and select **Graphics**. Alternatively, you can use the **Graphics panel** by clicking on **Graphic**s in the bottom right-right corner of the workspace.
- From the left drop-down list at the top of the panel, select from the categories of graphics
- From the lower-left, drop-down list at the top of the panel, select the type of art you want e.g., Background, Frames, Graphics, etc.
- Click on the graphics effect you want from the **Graphics panel**

The Blending Mode

A feature called the Blending Mode lets you select how colors will meld together when they overlap. The blend modes control how colors interact with one another in photos, layers, and even when you paint over a layer. You may quickly add, change, and remove blend modes from your image without having any impact on the image's pixels. There are a total of 25 blending modes.

The drop-down list at the top of the Layers panel in Expert Mode contains the blend modes. Keep in mind that the Photoshop Element has multiple locations where the blending modes can be found.

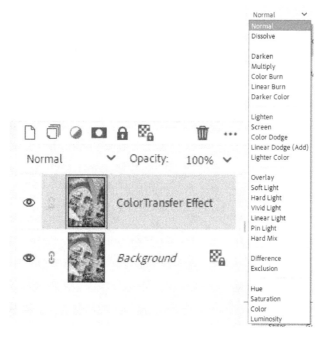

Let's examine the blending modes in each of their different categories now.

General Blend Modes

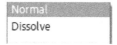

There are just two general blending modes. The first one is the default mode and is frequently utilized, whilst the second blending mode is the least popular.

- ↕ Normal
- ↕ Dissolve

Darken Blend Modes

The following modes are intended to add effects that darken your images:

- ✦ Darken
- ✦ Multiply
- ✦ Color Burn
- ✦ Linear Burn
- ✦ Darken Color

Lighten Blend Modes

Lighten
Screen
Color Dodge
Linear Dodge (Add)
Lighter Color

These blend modes help to add effects that brighten up your images and they are:

- ✦ Lighten
- ✦ Screen
- ✦ Color Dodge
- ✦ Linear Dodge
- ✦ Lighten Dodge
- ✦ Lighter Dodge
- ✦ Lighter Color

Contrast Blend Modes

Overlay
Soft Light
Hard Light
Vivid Light
Linear Light
Pin Light
Hard Mix

The Blending Modes in this category are a mixture of the Darken and the Lighten categories and they are:

- ✦ Overlay
- ✦ Soft Light
- ✦ Hard Light
- ✦ Vivid Light

- ▲ Linear Light
- ▲ Pin Light
- ▲ Hard Mix

Inversion Blend Modes

Difference
Exclusion

The Inversion Blending Modes look for variations between the base and blend layers to create the blend.

- ▲ Difference
- ▲ Exclusion

The Component Blend Modes

Hue
Saturation
Color
Luminosity

The Component Blending Modes use combinations of the primary color components (hue, saturation, and brightness) to create the blend.

- ▲ Hue
- ▲ Saturation
- ▲ Color
- ▲ Luminosity

CHAPTER SIXTEEN

TIPS AND TRICKS ON PHOTOSHOP ELEMENTS

We will discuss the hints and techniques that can be applied while using the Photoshop Element in this chapter. To foster a culture surrounding the use of the Photoshop Element, several tips and tricks are being introduced.

Let's now explore Photoshop Element's tricks and pointers.

Viewing An image In Two Windows

In the Photoshop Element, you can choose between two alternative views of an image. When you need to magnify an image to perform some detailed work, this capability can be useful. You might not be able to notice the impact of your edits on the image when it is zoomed in.

Go to the **View menu** and select **New Window** to view your image in two separate windows.

The image eventually displays in two windows after the instructions above are carried out.

Saving Your Selections With Your Photos

You can save each selection you've made while working on your image with the Save Selection function. You can access any selection you require in the future with this command.

Follow the procedures listed below to save a selection.

✦ Go to **Select** and click Save Selection

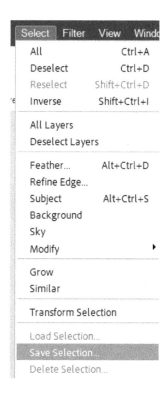

✦ In the **Save Selection** dialog box that pops up, set the selection to **New Selection** and then type in the name of your selection in the **Name box**

✦ Then click on **Ok**

♦ Once you've completed this, go to Select, click on Load Selection, and then select an option from the Selection drop-down menu to return to loading the saved selection.

Resetting A Dialog Box Without Closing It

By now, you should be aware that the dialog box is where the majority of Photoshop Element's adjustments are made. You might need to close the dialog box and reopen it to start over while making changes to it. Now you only need to click the Reset button instead of doing that. The Reset button, however, is still not always visible in dialog boxes. In these instances, all you need to do is press and hold the Alt key until the Cancel button changes to the Reset button.

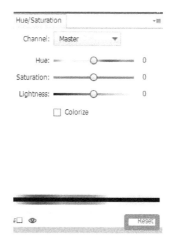

Changing The Ruler Unit Of Measurement

The Photoshop Element has several measurement units, including pixels, inches, centimeters, millimeters, points, picas, and %. Make sure that the ruler is visible before changing the unit of measurement; if it isn't, click **Ruler** on the **Menu bar's View** menu.

Right-click anywhere on the ruler after it appears at the top and left of your image to bring up a pop-up menu where you can select the unit of measurement you desire.

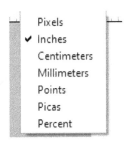

Having Access To Other Options In The Dialog Box

Do you know that, even when the dialog box is being utilized, you can still access other options?

When your dialog box opens, all you need to do is select **View** from the **menu**. Commands on the View menu that are fully black can be used, but those that are gray cannot.

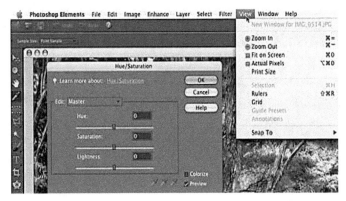

There are other settings available in the dialog box under the Window menu. Additionally, gray commands cannot be accessible, but all black instructions can.

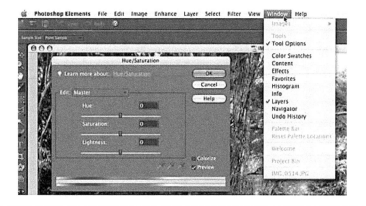

Viewing More Files In The Recently Edited List.

The list of the most recent 10 files you opened can be accessed similarly to the History panel. To view these files, select Recently Edited File from the File menu.

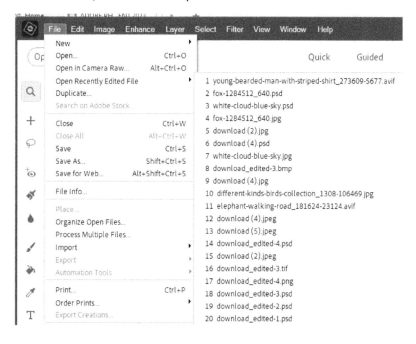

You can also view up to 30 files by going to the **Photoshop Elements Edit menu**, selecting **Preferences**, and then clicking on **Saving Files**, where you will adjust the figure to what you desire.

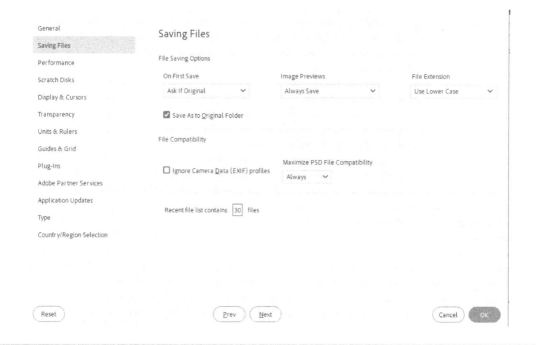

The Basic Shortcut Keys

Shortcut Result	Windows	Mac OS
Copy	Ctrl + C	Command + C
Cut	Ctrl + X	Command + X
Paste	Ctrl + V	Command + V
Delete	Del	Del
Duplicate	Alt + Up/down button	Option + Up/Down button
Deselect All	Ctrl + Shift + A	Command + Shift + Z
Undo	Ctrl + Z	Command + Z
Redo	Ctrl + Shift + Z	Command + Shift + Z
New	Ctrl + N	Command + N
Open	Ctrl + O	Command + O
Save	Ctrl + S	Command + S
Save As	Ctrl + Shift + S	Command + Shift + S
Save for Web	Alt + Ctrl + Shift + S	Command + Option + Shift + S
Export	Ctrl + E	Command + E
Deselect	Ctrl + D	Command + D

Shortcut Keys For Objects

Shortcut Result	Windows	Mac OS
Group	Ctrl + G	Command + G
Ungroup	Ctrl + Shift + G	Command + Shift+ G
Transform again	Ctrl + Alt + 4	Ctrl + Alt + 4
Centre to Content	Ctrl + Shift + E	Command + Shift + E
Text Frame Options	Ctrl +B	Ctrl + B

Shortcut Keys For Layout Menu

Shortcut Result	Windows	Mac OS
Go to Page	Ctrl + J	Command + J
Add Page	Ctrl + Shift +P	Command + Shift +P

Shortcut Keys For Arranging Layers

Shortcut Result	Windows	Mac OS
Bring to Font	Ctrl + Shift + [	Command + Shift + [
Send to Back	Ctrl + Shift +]	Command + Shift +]

View Menu Keyboard Shortcuts Keys

Shortcut Result	Windows	Mac OS
Smart Guides	Ctrl + U	Command + U
Text Threads	Ctrl + Alt + Y	Command + Alt + Y
Intersect	Ctrl + Alt +I	Command + Alt +I
Exclude Overlap	Ctrl + Alt + X	Command + Alt + X
Convert to Path	Ctrl + 8	Ctrl + 8

Shortcut Keys For Type Menu

Shortcut Result	Windows	Mac OS
Tabs	Shift + Ctrl + T	Shift + Command + T
Glyphs	Shift + Alt + F11	Shift + Options + F11

Shortcut keys For Zoom

Shortcut Result	Windows	Mac OS
Zoom (Drag mouse to Zoom)	Ctrl + Spacebar	Command + Spacebar
Zoom in/Zoom out	Ctrl + +/ Ctrl + -	Command+ +/ Command l + -
Pan in View	Spacebar + Drag	Spacebar + Drag
Fit Page in View	Ctrl + O	Command + O
Fit Spread in View	Ctrl + Option + O	Command + Option + O

Shortcut keys For Using Text

Shortcut Result	Windows	Mac OS
Move type in Image	Ctrl + Drag when the Type layer is selected	Command + Drag when the Type layer is selected.
Select 1 character left/right	Shift + Left Arrow/Right Arrow	Shift + Left Arrow/Right Arrow
Select 1 line down/up	Shift + Down Arrow/Up Arrow	Shift + Down Arrow/Up Arrow
Select 1 word left/right	Ctrl + Shift + Left Arrow/Right Arrow	Command+ Shift + Left Arrow/Right Arrow
Select characters from the insertion point to the mouse click point	Shift-click	Shift-click
Move 1 character left/right	Left Arrow/Right Arrow	Left Arrow/Right Arrow
Move 1 line down/up	Down Arrow/Up Arrow	Down Arrow/Up Arrow
Select 1 word left/right	Left Arrow/Right Arrow	Command + Left Arrow/Right Arrow
Select word	Double-click	Double-click
Select line	Triple-click	Triple-click
Select paragraph	Quadruple-click	Quadruple-click
Scale and skew text within a bounding	Control-drag a bounding box handle	Command-drag a bounding box handle

box when resizing the bounding box		
Align top or bottom	Vertical Type tool or R	Vertical Type tool or R
Align center	Vertical Type Mask tool + Control + Shift + L, C	Vertical Type Mask tool + Control + Shift + L, C
Return to the default font style	Ctrl + Shift + Y	Command + Shift + Y
Turn Underlining on/off	Ctrl +Shift + U	Command +Shift + U
Turn Strikethrough on/ off	Ctrl + Shift + /	Command + Shift + /
Decrease or increase the type size of selected text 1 pt/px	Ctrl + Shift + < or >	Command + Shift + < or >

Shortcut keys For Selecting And Moving Objects

Shortcut Result	Windows	Mac OS
Deselect a selection	Ctrl + D	Command + D
Reposition the marquee while selecting	Spacebar-drag	Spacebar-drag
Add to or subtract from a selection	Any selection tool + Shift or Alt-drag	Any selection tool + Shift or Option-drag
Intersect a selection	Any selection tool (excluding Quick Selection tool and Selection Brush tool)+ Shift + Alt-drag	Any selection tool (excluding Quick Selection tool and Selection Brush tool) + Shift + Alt-drag
Constrain marquee to square or circle If no other selections are active	Shift-drag	Shift-drag
Draw a marquee from the center (If no other selections are active)	Alt-drag	Option-drag

Constrain shape and draw marquee from the center	Shift + Alt-drag	Shift + Option-drag
Switch to Move tool	Control (except when Hand or any shape tool is selected)	Command (except when Hand or any shape tool is selected)
Switch from the Magnetic Lasso tool to the Polygonal Lasso tool	Alt-click and drag	Option-click and drag
Delete the last anchor point for the Magnetic or Polygonal lasso tool	Delete	Delete
Apply an operation of the Magnetic Lasso tool	Enter	Enter
Cancel an operation of the Magnetic Lasso tool	Esc	Esc
Move a copy of a selection	Move tool +Alt-drag selection	Move tool +Option-drag selection
Move selection area 1 pixel	Move tool + Right Arrow, Left Arrow, Up Arrow, or Down Arrow	Move tool + Right Arrow, Left Arrow, Up Arrow, or Down Arrow
Move layer 1 pixel when nothing is selected on layer	Control + Right Arrow, Left Arrow, Up Arrow, or Down Arrow	Command + Right Arrow, Left Arrow, Up Arrow, or Down Arrow
Increase/decrease detection width	Magnetic Lasso tool + [or]	Magnetic Lasso tool + [or]
Accept cropping or exit cropping	Crop tool + Enter or Esc	Crop tool + Enter or Esc
Toggle the crop shield off and on	(forward slash) /	/ (forward slash)

Shortcut Keys For layers Panel

Shortcut Result	Windows	Mac OS
Set layer options	Alt-click New button	Option-click New button
Delete without confirmation	Alt-click Trash button	Option-click Trash button
Apply value and keep the text box active	Shift + Enter	Shift + Enter
Load layer transparency as a selection	Control-click layer thumbnail	Command-click layer thumbnail
Add to the current selection	Ctrl + Shift-click	Command + Shift-click layer thumbnail
Subtract from the current selection	Ctrl +Shift + Alt-click layer thumbnail	Command +Shift + Alt-click layer thumbnail
Intersect with the current selection	Ctrl + Shift + Alt-click layer thumbnail	Command + Shift + Option-click layer thumbnail
Merge layers	Ctrl + Shift + E	Command + Shift + E
Create a new empty layer with a dialog	Alt-click the New Layer button	Option-click the New Layer button
Create a new layer below the target layer	Control-click the New Layer button	Command-click the New Layer button
Activate the bottom/top layer	Alt + .(period)/ ,(comma)	Option + .(period)/ ,(comma)
Select the next layer down/up	Alt + [or]	Option + [or]
Move the target layer down/up	Ctrl + [or]	Command + [or]
Merge a copy of all visible layers into the target layer	Ctrl + Shift + Alt + E	Command + Shift + Option + E
Merge down	Ctrl + E	Command + E

304

Copy the current layer to the layer below	Alt + Merge Down command from the panel pop-up menu	Option + Merge Down command from the panel pop-up menu
Copy all visible layers to the active layer	Alt + Merge Visible command from the panel pop-up menu	Option + Merge Visible command from the panel pop-up menu
Show/hide all other currently visible layers	Alt-click the eye icon	Option-click the eye icon
Toggle lock transparency for the target layer, or the last applied lock	/ (forward slash)	/ (forward slash)
Select all text; temporarily select the Type tool	Double-click the text layer thumbnail	Double-click the text layer thumbnail
Create a clipping mask	Alt-click the line dividing the two layers	Option-click the line dividing the two layers
Rename layer	Double-click the layer name	Double-click the layer name
Add to layer selection in the Layers panel	Shift + Alt + [or]	Shift + Option + [or]
Copy the mask from one layer to another, and ask to replace it if the mask is already present	Alt + drag layer mask	Alt + drag layer mask

Shortcut Keys For Painting And Brushing

Shortcut Result	Windows	Mac OS
Switch to the Eyedropper tool	Any painting tool or shape tool + Alt (except Impressionist Brush)	Any painting tool or shape tool + Alt (except Impressionist Brush)
Select background-color	Eyedropper tool + Alt-click	Eyedropper tool + Option-click

Set opacity, tolerance, or exposure for the painting	Any painting or editing tool + number keys. When the airbrush option is enabled, use the Shift + number keys.	Any painting or editing tool + number keys. When the airbrush option is enabled, use the Shift + number keys.
Cycle through blending mode	Shift + + (plus) or - (minus)	Shift + + (plus) or - (minus)
Fill selection/layer with foreground or background color	Alt + Backspace, or Ctrl + Backspace	Option + Delete (Backspace), or Command + Delete (Backspace)
Display Fill dialog box	Shift + Backspace	Shift + Delete (Backspace)
Lock transparent pixels on/off	/ (forward slash)	/ (forward slash)
Connect points with a straight line (draw a straight line)	Any painting tool + Shift-click	Any painting tool + Shift-click
Delete brush	Alt-click brush	Option-click brush
Decrease/increase brush size	[or]	[or]
Decrease/increase brush softness/hardness in 25% increments	Shift + [or]	Shift + [or]
Select the previous/next brush size	, (comma) or. (period)	, (comma) or. (period)
Select the first/last brush	Shift +, (comma) or. (period)	Shift +, (comma) or. (period)
Display precise crosshair for brushes	Caps Lock	Caps Lock

CHAPTER SEVENTEEN

TROUBLESHOOTING IN PHOTOSHOP ELEMENTS 2024

Without a doubt, one of Adobe's improved tools with unique features is Photoshop Element. However, one or two issues will unavoidably arise.

In this chapter of the book, I'll be highlighting several potential problems and offering fixes.

Handling Catalog Issues

Your images and other relevant media files' information is kept in a database called the catalog in the Photoshop Element. The catalog is automatically stored on the computer's hard drive.

Optimizing Your Catalog

By making your catalog more efficient, you may decrease the amount of space it takes up while simultaneously improving its functionality. The following procedures can help you optimize your catalog.

Ensure that Photoshop Element Editor is shut down.

- ✦ Go to **File** and click on **Manage Catalogs**

- ✦ When the **Catalog Manager** dialog box is displayed, select the catalog to be optimized, and then click on **Optimize.**

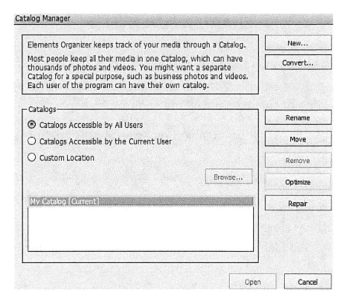

✦ After this finishes loading, you will be notified, then click on **Ok** to close

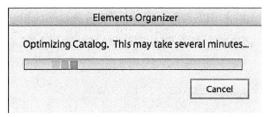

To solve thumbnail issues in the Element Organizer, optimizing the catalog is a sure way.

Repairing Your Catalog

You could run across issues while using Photoshop Element that results in harm to the catalog file.

The steps listed below should be used to repair damaged catalogs.

✦ Go to File and click on Manage Catalogs

- When the Catalog Manager dialog box is displayed, select the catalog to repair, and then click on Repair

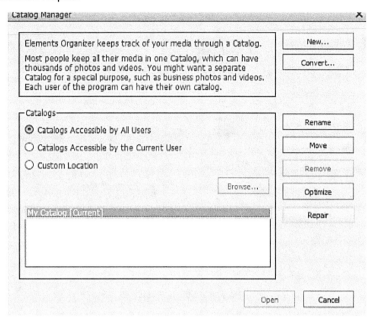

- Here, the Photoshop Element checks the errors, when this is done, mark the **Re-index Visual Similarity Data** and then click on **Repairs Anyway**

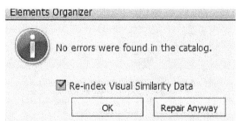

- After completing this process, click on **Ok** to exit the dialog box.

Save As Format such as JPEG are missing

If you want to save your file as a JPEG, Photoshop Element's Save As command only shows PSD, PSD, and TIFF. When you find yourself in a situation like this, save files in formats like JPEG, PNG, PDF, etc. by using the Save A Copy option.

To locate the Save A Copy,

- Select **Save As** from the **File** Menu
- Click on **Save A Copy** from under the **Save As** dialog box.

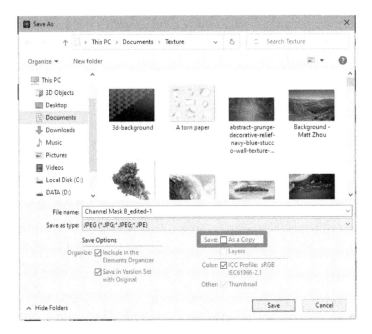

- ✦ Selecting Save a Copy allows you to use other saving file formats as shown in the image below.

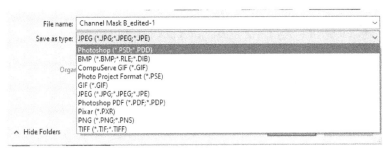

Adjusting Dates For Different Time Zones

When you have an inaccurate date, it can interfere with your photo search in Photoshop Element. You can end up with erroneous search results even if your time and the time zone are both right.

Follow the procedures below to adjust the date for different time zones:

- ✦ Open the **Organizer** and choose the files whose dates you want to modify.
- ✦ To change the date and time, right-click the image and then choose **Adjust Date and Time.**

In the **Adjust Date and Time of Selected Item** dialog box, click on **Shift by a set of hours (time zone adjust)**

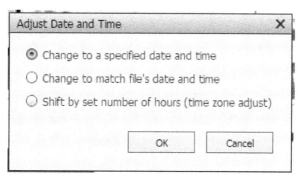

In the Time Zone Adjust dialog box, specify the time interval based on **Ahead** or **Back** options and then click on Ok.

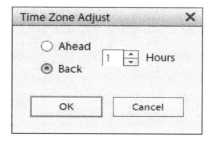

Finding Lost/Disconnected Files

One issue with Photoshop Element is that it can cause lost or disconnected files. But before we discover how to rejoin lost files, let's look at the reasons why files detach. One or more of the following factors could be the reason for your missing or disconnected files.

- Erasing files using programs other than Photoshop Element, such as Windows Explorer.
- Renaming the files with Windows Explorer or other products besides Photoshop Element
- Moving files from one location to another through Windows Explorer or other programs besides Photoshop Element
- Formatting the hard drive and transferring the files to a different window account with a unique name.

The connection between the thumbnail and the actual master image is severed when all these things take place.

Follow the instructions below to find any missing files in your organizer:

- Open a folder in your **Organizer,** then choose the disconnected or missing file. (A tiny circle on the file's corner serves as a marker for any missing files.).

- Select **Reconnect** from the **File** Menu And then click on **Missing File.**

The Photoshop Element is attempting to find the missing here on this page. If you are aware of the location of the lost file, click **Browse** to find it.

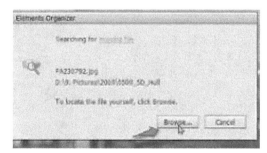

In the **Reconnect Missing File**s dialog box, click on the Folder that has the missing file and the missing file will be displayed at the right-hand side of the dialog box under **Locate the Missing File**

Then click on **Reconnect to** restore the missing file

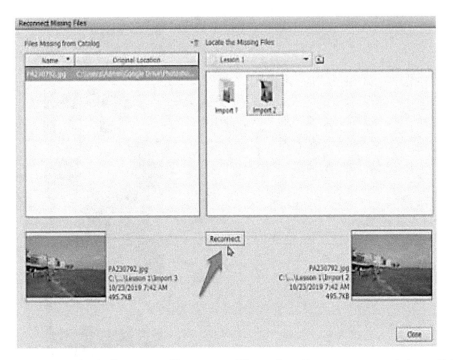

In case you need to find all missing files, go to **File,** select **Reconnect,** and then click on **All Missing Files.** This process may take some time but once it has been done, all the missing files will be reconnected.

CONCLUSION

Having gone through this manual guide, I am sure you must have learned many things about Photoshop Element 2024.

Also, by now, you must have realized that with this user guide, learning how to use Photoshop Element with various versions up to date is as easy as ABC.

Finally, you can recommend this user guide to your friends and family to enjoy what you have enjoyed.

See you around later!

INDEX

318

319

www.ingramcontent.com/pod-product-compliance
Lightning Source LLC
LaVergne TN
LVHW081515050326
832903LV00025B/1503